Divorcing and Healing from a Narcissist

How to Heal From a Narcissist after a Divorce

Martina Roswell

Table of Contents

Introduction 1

Chapter One Marriage With A Narcissist 5

Chapter Two Emotional And Narcissistic Abuse 27

Chapter Three Narcissistic Love Bombing And Hate Bombing 45

Chapter Four The Exhausted Spouse 55

Chapter Five Divorcing A Narcissist: The Utter Hell 65

Chapter Six Mind Games Narcissists Play 87

Chapter Seven Life After Divorce From A Narcissist 103

Chapter Eight Emotional Survival 111

Chapter Nine Safeguarding Yourself 127

Chapter Ten Moving On After Divorce From A Narcissist 143

Chapter Eleven Trauma Recovery 155

Chapter Twelve Mistakes Preventing Healing 173

Chapter Thirteen Co-Parenting With A Narcissist 179

Chapter Fourteen Finding Yourself 193

Chapter Fifteen The Mirror Theory 197

Chapter Sixteen When It Is Over 203

Conclusion 211

Introduction

You must have suffered in the hands of a narcissist through the years. You know, that person who thinks they are so great and won't keep quiet about it. You find them always talking about their latest and greatest achievement, always talking about how they are hotter than everyone in the room; you know, that person who sees themselves as smarter than everyone else. They always find a way to revert every ongoing conversation with someone back to themself.

The narcissist is someone who hides behind a "false self". Their false self is made up of traits they show to the world as who they are, and they do this to gain attention and admiration.

They are so weird that they can believe that they are gifted at a particular skill when in the real sense of it, they truly don't possess that skill. A narcissist who is poor at writing may see themself as equal to William Shakespeare.

They can be so self-deluded that they can even think they are so perfect that they don't need an editor for their write-up. Tell them the truth about their lack of the skill and watch them prove they can do it by doing it again, and ending up with even more tragic results than they first did.

Even though narcissists can stubbornly believe that they possess a skill they clearly don't possess, and they won't stop torturing those around by using the non-existent talent, they actually possess some real talents.

What about those skills they truly have? The world can be made better if narcissists can focus on their skills and not ignore them.

If narcissists with verbal eloquence can stop trying to be the writers or painters they are not and focus on helping their countries negotiate great deals for progress and growth, the world would be a more productive and much better place for us all to live in.

Narcissists are naturally dependent on others for their emotional survival, actively pursuing others for their narcissistic supply.

If narcissists can focus on their strengths, and not neglect them, the world would have been much better, but they just won't.

Now, enough about them! What about you? How do you feel about your partner's grandiosity? Your narcissistic sweetheart has had your heart broken 10,000 times, but they don't even feel you are hurt. Even though you may not be physically abused in the relationship, they still manage to make your life a living hell by their emotionally abusive and must-win-every-argument behavior.

You think of yourself as a strong person who can handle your partner's behavior, but the truth of the matter is that you are simply living in denial. The strength you think you have is not really strength; it is denial.

The narcissist's actions are quite predictable. They are so emotionally bankrupt that they never want to experience any emotion that will not promote their grandiosity. Because of this behavior of theirs, they go through life emotionally shortchanging everyone.

You must be able to identify with someone's pain for you to show empathy for their situation. Unfortunately, narcissists do not have the capability to identify with their partners' pain.

You give and give and give, and your narcissist takes and takes and takes from you. You keep showering them with love and affection, but they never reciprocate any of the good things you do for them.

In the subsequent chapters of this book, we will be discussing divorce and how you can heal from the pains inflicted on you by your partner's narcissistic behavior.

CHAPTER ONE

Marriage with a Narcissist

All the signs of narcissism are not quite obvious. A lot of people have different traits of narcissism, but they don't even know it. Everyone has one or two of the narcissistic trait. They have these traits without being full-blown narcissists or being diagnosed with narcissistic personality disorder.

Narcissism exists on a spectrum of severity, and only a qualified mental health professional can make an official diagnosis to ascertain if a person is a narcissist or not.

You won't go ahead to marry a narcissist on purpose, but they have excellent trickery and manipulation skills. Their personality disorder sees them having a grandiose sense of self-importance.

Living with a narcissistic spouse can be a very painful and frustrating experience, especially because they are someone close to your heart. You are face to face with your loved one's lack of concern for your feelings, and their excessive self-centeredness makes you wonder how you even got along with them in the first place.

Being married to a narcissist has left you struggling with an almost non-existent intimate relationship because your partner's narcissistic behavior is a characterological disorder that is extremely difficult to cure.

They are always right, and you are always wrong. They are always perfect, and you are always the one with mistakes and flaws. They find faults with everything, even when you are incredibly good.

Even though empathy is a necessary aspect of living that helps us to be sensitive to other people's feelings and be compassionate towards them, a narcissist has no empathy. Your marriage to your partner is supposed to be the most important relationship in your life, but your partner is simply incapable of having a real intimate relationship.

The Mental Illness

Marriage on its own without the added stress of a narcissistic partner's behavior is challenging. Life is complicated when living with a partner who has a mental health condition. The relationship doesn't get better; its complexity increases.

Finding yourself stuck in this situation, you might be wondering what next to do to get yourself unstuck.

How can you be valuable to a partner with an inflated sense of self-importance, and an unending need for admiration and excessive attention?

They may have a lack of empathy for others and wear a mask of extreme confidence, but behind this mask hides a fragile self-esteem that can be shattered with the slightest criticism.

Narcissists feel disappointed and unhappy when people don't recognize them and give them the kind of admiration or special favors they crave and believe they deserve. People with this personality disorder cause many problems in different areas of life, such as their workplace or school. They may even experience problems with their financial affairs.

People with narcissistic personality disorder may be generally unhappy and disappointed when they're not given the special favors or admiration they believe they deserve. Other people may not enjoy spending time with them because of their personality disorder, so they may find themselves having unfulfilling relationships.

Symptoms of Narcissistic Personality Disorder

The signs and symptoms associated with a narcissistic personality disorder vary, and the severity of the symptoms also varies. The following are noticed in people with narcissistic personality disorder:

- They have an exaggerated belief of self-importance.

- They have a sense of entitlement and a deep need for excessive admiration and adoration.
- They exaggerate their talents and achievements and expect to be recognized as superior, even if their achievements are nothing special.
- They believe they are superior and can only be connected with equally exceptional people.
- They are preoccupied with fantasies about success, prestige, power, vanity, brilliance, or beauty.
- They make conversations all about themselves and belittle or look down on those they believe as inferior to them.
- They insist on having the very best and don't mind taking advantage of others to have their way and get what they want.
- They lack empathy and are unable and unwilling to recognize the needs and feelings of others.
- They envy others but believe others are envying them.
- They are arrogant, boastful, and pretentious.

People with this disorder have been known to have trouble handling criticism, and they can:

- Get impatient and angry when they are not given special treatment.

- Have challenges with controlling their emotions and behavior.
- React by belittling someone who has criticized them; they do this to make themselves appear superior.
- Find it really difficult dealing with stress and changes.
- Experience moodiness and depression if they fall short of perfection.
- Experience secret feelings of vulnerability, insecurity, humility, and shame.

You know that your partner has a personality disorder, but they are unaware that they do. They are not only unaware that they are narcissistic; they may even think you are the one who is the narcissist if they read the signs of the disorder above.

If your partner has many of these signs, then know that it won't be easy divorcing them, since they always feel that they are the ones who should leave their partner, and not the other way round.

Double Standards

Narcissists have double standards. They live in a self-constructed world of distortions. They set different standards for themselves than the ones they set for others.

This double standard behavior of theirs is confusing. It can make dealing with them frustrating and energy draining.

Despite all their shortcomings and hurtful manipulations, they see themselves as perfect. They belittle their spouse, children, siblings, and other family members.

You become the answer to their dreams, and they stay attached to you once they notice that you can do something to fatten their pocketbook or boost their image. As soon as they have gotten what they wanted from you, they quickly discard you in exchange for the next person that they feel can fulfill their new desire.

Marriage with them is challenging because they are incapable of having any real relationship and making it work. No matter how many times you may overlook things, stay strong, and try to make the marriage work, they continue to give you endless troubles until divorcing and severing contact with this disturbed individual becomes a recurring thought in your mind.

The process of divorce is often difficult and never easy. It requires a lot of determination and perseverance. After divorcing your partner, you find yourself enjoying your freedom as you used to before you got married to them, and you return to the driver's seat of your life and regain control; your creativity increases as well as your inner peace.

Narcissists act the way they want, but they don't allow others the freedom to act the way they want; they deny them the opportunity to do so.

Their double standards make it exhausting for those around them. It is necessary for us to discuss some of the double standards narcissists hold.

Narcissists tend to have some key paradoxes; let us discuss these paradoxes.

They Are Hypersensitive but Insensitive

At the smallest perceived slight, narcissists act like the martyr. They often like to be the center of attention and have their way at all times, so they sulk when this is not the case.

They often ignore the needs of others and ridicule them in times of crisis. They are quick to get irritated with requests for help and may even label the person asking them for help "demanding".

Their actions have negative consequences, which causes unbearable pain for those close to them. When those actions are pointed out by those around them, they act mystified or even clueless about it.

They Are Oppositional but Don't Tolerate Opposition

Narcissists tend to say no or oppose what others say.

They seem to be energized by doing that, and it almost looks as if they enjoy the opportunity to ruin the mood of others.

A narcissist is always blaming someone else for their misfortune. They never get tired of doing that. A relationship has problems, and then they turn the table around and point an accusing finger to their spouse as the reason for the failing relationship. For them, it's about your incompetence and how your behavior made them react in a certain manner.

They can seek revenge and pursue legal action, yet when someone calls them to account for their own wrongdoings, they can become so full of disbelief that anyone would dare to oppose them. It can result in them personally attacking the person or making them their enemy.

They Are Demanding Of Attention, yet They Don't Reciprocate It

Narcissists are lovers of attention. They can go to any length to get the attention they desire. They can switch to negative behavior just so that they can remain relevant if positive behavior is not putting them in the spotlight and giving them the attention they crave.

Despite the fact that they love affirmation and admiration, they withhold it from others. The only reason they listen to people talk about themselves sometimes is because they're waiting impatiently for the conversation to be focused back on them.

You'll find them competing even with their loved one as if their loved one's win takes something away from them.

They Are Charming Outside, But Hellish At Home

Narcissists appear charming and may be great-hearted to outsiders. Outsiders may perceive them as perfect, but when they return home, they show off their worst behaviors. They become what the public doesn't know about them. They become selfish or bully their spouse.

They Pick Fights But Are Defensive

Narcissists seem defined by oppositions as they always seem to have an enemy. They pick fights easily, yet no one dares to question them. They get enraged when people challenge them.

Righteous but Brittle

Narcissists tend to sink into despair if they feel humiliated. They have a right or wrong, white and black view of the world. Their personality sees them being obsessed with cleanliness, details, rules, order, or schedules.

They Are Hungry For Attention, But Stingy In Sharing the Spotlight

A narcissist's drug of choice is attention. They usually get impatient when others are talking about anything other than them until they can steer the conversation back to themselves. While they love standing out and getting noticed by everyone around, they deny others a chance to stand out and shine.

A narcissist may delight in ruining someone's mood if the person is in a good mood, and they are not. It almost seems like it is the narcissist's loss when anything good and positive happens to someone other than them.

They Are Emotionally Demanding but Clueless

Narcissists seem unaware of the pain they cause those around them. They sulk and take up all the emotional air in a room and then act clueless or blameless after ruining a family holiday that was full of fun.

Dealing with narcissists can be mystifying; never expect fairness, compassion, or reciprocity from them.

You will find their behavior less puzzling once you realize that they have issues with their self-esteem and are constantly fighting off threats to it. This realization will help you not to take their actions personally.

Walking On Eggshells

Have you ever thought for a minute about walking on eggshells? Chances are you would tread lightly and won't be walking relaxed. You would be tensed and trying to walk without breaking the eggshells or even hurt your feet by walking on that.

Now relate this to your relationship. Whenever your partner is around, you seem to be walking on eggshells because you never know what mood they may be in. You tread lightly first to see their reaction before you can know how to behave around them or what to say to them.

Your pattern of tiptoeing around them to first study their mood is referred to as walking on eggshells. You are always careful with what you say and do around them. You find it difficult relaxing because you are fearful of being criticized, abused, and chastised for not meeting their expectations; this leaves you constantly feeling like you are walking on eggshells.

You have the feeling that you can get summoned at any moment to have a discussion about things you have done wrong, how you have disappointed them, and how you haven't met their expectations of you. They communicate by using aggression to express anger over issues; this can be dragged further and can even lead to physical abuse.

They often view you as an object that is there just to meet all their needs and expectations, so when you don't meet their expectations, they blame and criticize you for that. It's this behavior of theirs that is making you tense as you are always expecting the next confrontation or outburst.

It's not a good sign when you have to walk on eggshells around your partner. Each day you wake up, you always tread lightly because your partner displays simply toxic traits. You keep trying to avoid them lashing out at you at every given opportunity because their moods and outbursts are unpredictable. The littlest of things can trigger their anger and outburst, and you never know what to expect next. They overreact to issues that shouldn't be blown out of proportion.

Most times, the relationship anxiety you feel is high because the relationship can switch to conflict or something toxic so fast without you being prepared for it. At the drop of a hat, things can change, so you are careful not to change the atmosphere of a peaceful moment. Their fragile mood scares you, making you feel like the ground you walk on is unstable.

Because of your partner's narcissistic behavior, you will go out of your way to have peace in the relationship, even if the peace comes at your own disadvantage.

Do you tread lightly and hesitate to interact with your spouse because of this behavior of theirs? If you do, you are "walking on eggshells".

This Is Emotional Abuse, and we should call it what it is. We don't have to come up with different names to make it less bad; it is what it is; emotional abuse. You may call it walking on eggshells or treading lightly, but it's still abuse.

Self-doubt gradually sets in when you are a victim of emotional abuse. Your partner abuses you to the point where you become unsure of the situation. Sometimes you are sure that what they are doing is wrong for a healthy marriage, and then at some other times, you get confused and feel the complete opposite.

You're afraid of your partner's response to situations, so you walk on eggshells. Their moods and behavior are unstable, and even they themselves cannot predict what their response to situations would be.

On some days, they may stay quiet and let some things pass without getting upset. But there are other days when they overreact and blow very little things out of proportion; this makes you keep your issues to yourself, and you avoid admitting whenever you have done something wrong because they would overreact.

You also avoid telling them any bad news. You find yourself covering up little things that shouldn't even be issues, just to avoid your partner's outburst whenever you are honest.

The Silent Treatment: When Your Narcissist Shuts Up

Narcissists use the silent treatment as a weapon. Sometimes, the mere absence of communication hurts more than words. The narcissist uses the silent treatment to silence their partner because they know that silence is a powerful weapon.

It is a passive-aggressive communication style that is used to convey disapproval and displeasure. Once you confront a narcissist about something they have done wrong, they use this silence technique to place the blame for the situation on you and never take responsibility for their wrongful behavior.

If your partner has used this weapon of silence to punish you, you should already be familiar with it and know that it is a form of emotional abuse. You are unable to defend yourself or explain things to resolve the conflict once they shut down all forms of communication with you. Deep down inside of you, you know it isn't right, and you want to make things right, but there is nothing you can do because they have already shut their mouth and won't talk to you.

Narcissistic partners use this technique to maintain control over their spouses if they dare to react with the assertion of their boundaries. They use silent treatment to punish them for the perceived assault against their ego. Their silent treatment is a painful weapon that is meant to disintegrate the victim's worth.

You experience the same neurological response as physical pain when you are experiencing the silent treatment.

Our brain responds to the emotional abuse of rejection in just the same manner in which it responds to physical pain. During the period you are experiencing the silent treatment from your partner, what happens is that painful demands are sent into your conscious self by screaming neurons to identify what is causing you the pain, and to stop it. They tell you to return to the person who is causing you the pain. When you are experiencing rejection from silent treatment, the sensation that your brain feels is the same as physical pain. Emotional abuse, in this case, is just like physical abuse.

You feel the same pain as if you were being hit physically, so you get so desperate to have them end the silent treatment and talk to you again.

Our brains are naturally designed to crave the affection and approval of others because we are social creatures. Narcissists understand this fact, so they deny you attention to have power over you. You are turned into nothing with the silent treatment they give you because to become invisible is to become nothing. The silent treatment is used to punish, silence, and control you. The chronic use of the silent treatment is emotional abuse because you suffer emotional pain from it.

Questioning Reality

Gaslighting is when you are manipulated into questioning and second-guessing what you already know as your reality. Manipulating people use this tactic a lot. They use it to gain power over someone else. Narcissists act like a puppet master, and this makes you the victim of their actions.

Gaslighting has several stages, and it can be difficult for the victim to find out what is happening because it happens gradually over time. It can start with something like some little lies here and there and then gradually builds up from there, and you never realize what is happening in time.

Narcissists may tell lies about situations that you know they are telling lies about, but they will still get angry that you are questioning them. You will even find them denying that they ever said or did something you are sure that they said or did. Once they keep doing this, you start doubting yourself, questioning your reality, and then accepting theirs as the truth.

They may even compliment you every now and then to make you feel good about yourself until you start questioning whether they are really bad like you think. All of these leave you more confused, and you start thinking that you are beginning to lose your mind.

Narcissists can also create more distance between you and those you trust. They can tell them that you are losing your mind and then come back to tell you that you shouldn't see those people anymore. They can use your friends against you.

You can see your reality being canceled, there is chaos and confusion, everything that used to be straight is now upside down, and you don't know what to believe. However, you must realize that when psychological abuse distorts the truth and manipulation erases your reality, you can still survive it.

Your narcissist partner doesn't ask you about how your day went, and they don't even wish you a good day when you are leaving the house. The things you are working on are none of their business, and they show no concern about them unless they are things they equally care about.

You will miss your partner and wait for them all the time, but they won't reciprocate your love; this will make you feel stuck in the relationship, and it will be difficult for you to leave when you want to. You will make them experience your good behavior while they project their own bad behaviors onto you.

Your partner calls you a lunatic when their crazy behavior finally brings you to your breaking point, and you refuse to take it anymore. Others around will also start thinking that you are truly a lunatic. You will even start believing that about yourself.

Everyone will believe that about you, and no one will see the truth except maybe the kids who have been paying attention to everything that has been going on. The entire experience can result in trauma, which in turn causes you to question your reality.

You begin to feel crazy, and then numb, and then you question your reality. Realize that you do not have a problem with your marriage; it is your partner who has a mental illness.

Never Say No

No is the one word a narcissist never wants to hear anyone say to them. They find it very difficult to accept criticism and won't take no for an answer. The last time you tried to say no to your partner, you stopped yourself from saying it before they overreact to your response and blow it out of proportion. You can't say no to their style of doing things; the last time someone else even tried to tell them, they asked them never to talk to them in that manner again.

Narcissists have many words that really get them angry that they don't want to hear, but the worst of the words involve a "no". They hate to hear people tell them things like, "no, you're wrong", and worst of all, "no, I can't". Therefore it becomes difficult for you to relate with them properly.

You can't even have normal social interactions with them because you are not sure of what will trigger their anger. If you dare to challenge them, you risk suffering the silent treatment from them and getting punished for saying no.

Saying no isn't a bad thing. Learn to say no to unreasonable or impossible requests as they will get you ready to say yes to the really important things you should be saying yes to.

The Narcissist: The Human Parasite

A parasite is an organism that lives on or in a host and benefits by deriving its food from the host at its expense.

Narcissists rely on others as a means of supply, so understanding narcissism through the lens of parasitism explains the reliance better.

Narcissists suffer from a destabilized identity and a sense of inferiority, and their adaptation style is by projecting a superior persona. They are always busy seeking the validation they didn't receive at crucial development stages of their life. They have an incomplete sense of being, which makes them connect with people of high status to boost their self-worth. They also separate themselves from people who threaten the false persona they have created for themselves.

Narcissists control their suppliers through manipulations, bullying, silent treatment, and other hurtful behaviors. They orchestrate the reality around them by enlisting others in supporting their delusions and rejecting the people who don't give in to their demands.

When their spouse questions their opinion of something they have declared the truth, they see it as a humiliation and react with anger because their ego is threatened. The narcissist, who is the human parasite, drains their host physically, emotionally, and psychologically.

Narcissists are good at finding and attaching themselves to people they perceive as potential hosts. They pick out hosts who have qualities like, being well-liked, famous, wealthy, professionally accomplished, or even good looking. The host even supports the narcissist in accomplishing their goals by tolerating their abusive behavior, thereby serving the needs of the narcissist at their own expense.

Are you a narcissist's host? Here are some ways to find out:

- Your partner demands excessive attention and admiration, and reacts bitterly or creates a scene if they feel ignored.
- Your partner reacts with rage if you argue with them or disagree with their opinion.
- Your partner never apologizes for their inappropriate or hurtful behavior towards you.
- Your partner shows no compassion for your feelings, and their bad behaviors are projected onto you.
- You are constantly being attacked or criticized in the marriage, so you suppress your feelings to avoid confrontation.
- You are highly vigilant to potential conflict, and you feel isolated in the marriage.

CHAPTER TWO

Emotional and Narcissistic Abuse

Partners of people with narcissistic mental illness suffer narcissistic abuse, which is the scary new kind of emotional abuse.

You have experienced their self-absorbed behavior firsthand and understand that they think they are totally better and more important than everyone else.

Narcissists may be casually self-obsessed or even deeply pathological. They come in many forms, and their feelings and desires are the only things that matter to them.

Living with them means you must have undergone so much suffering and become the victim of narcissistic abuse. They lie to you all the time and even make it seem like it was your fault if you even dared to ask them why something happened. They are unrelenting about their need to be first and to be noticed.

Emotional abuse committed by a narcissist is referred to as narcissistic abuse, and emotional abuse is something you don't want to experience as it can be painful to endure.

Emotional abuse can be in different forms. It can be your abuser trying to manipulate and control you, or it might be them constantly checking to know your whereabouts. It might also be them insulting, threatening or even cheating on you and blaming you for it.

Your partner will make you feel like you are the one who is crazy and not them. They will get you confused by making you feel like you are imagining events and conversations inaccurately. They aim to make you reliant on the relationship.

Some people still go on to have healthy relationships with a narcissist and may not suffer emotional abuse from them. While some people don't suffer in the relationship with their narcissistic partner, some others are drained of self and life. The more narcissistic a person is, the more suffering their partner will go through.

What to Do

You can talk to a mental health professional if you are dealing with a narcissistic partner who puts you through emotional abuse. You may be able to save the marriage, but there are instances where you may not be able to save the marriage and will need to part ways with your spouse.

Relationships are a two-way street, so you shouldn't be married to someone who takes up all the air in the room. Your emotional health will suffer terribly if you are married to such a person.

It may be quite hard to actually have many good things to say about being married to a narcissist, but narcissism could be a positive trait when expressed as self-esteem and confidence. However, when expressed as control and arrogance, it becomes negative and not good.

Whatever you intend to do next, know that you can get help for your situation and you don't have to try to carry your problems alone. Partners of narcissists need lots of support to help them find themselves and stay sane.

Red Flags

Remember the feeling you get when you and your partner fight over the same issue over and over again? It's now about the 50th time, and you're still having yet another high-drama argument with them over the same thing, and there is nothing you can do to make it stop completely.

When arguments like this keep coming up, you just know deep down that there is something terribly wrong with your partner, but you're just trying to keep things on the low by keeping the volume down. You don't want to refer to their behavior as emotional abuse.

You can usually spot the signs of a toxic relationship from the beginning when you are both starting out. You had the gut instinct, but you ignored the signs and moved on with the relationship. Ignoring the signs was a big mistake. There was a deep-seated feeling telling you that the relationship isn't right for you. How can you be blamed for everything all the time? How can you always be wrong and never right? You should have followed your instinct.

The emotional and psychological abuse inflicted on someone by a person with Narcissistic Personality Disorder is referred to as Narcissistic abuse.

If you don't break free from the toxic relationship, the narcissistic abuse can cause you irreparable emotional damage.

Signs of Narcissism

Selfish and Lacks Empathy

Habitually disregarding your feelings and needs is something a narcissist partner is good at doing. They are only concerned about what others can do for them, so they don't really care about you. They seem to have mastered the ability to use others for their own personal gain. They will show you acts of kindness if it is to their advantage. For them, life is all about them.

Their contradictory behavior leaves you confused because you start thinking about all the bad behavior they show towards you and then turning around to become nice to you only because it will be to their advantage. You now realize that they can actually behave well, but they are deliberately choosing not to.

Egotistical and Arrogant

Something is definitely not right if your spouse always expects to be seen as superior and adored without any noteworthy accomplishments on their part. Some of the achievements they talk about or even the hero stories they tell may even not be true. They may be merely fabricated stories just to make them feel superior and important.

It is interesting to see them seek to spend time around other people whom they believe are equally important and worthy of their self-proclaimed supremacy.

Insatiable Need for Approval and Adoration

If your spouse constantly needs you to praise them, tell them how much of a genius they are, and gifted at everything than everyone around, then you must have noticed the pattern of them always needing an ego boost. They need to feed their desire for status, power, intellect, and significance.

Asserts Power And Dominance

Narcissists are control freaks because they are trying to cover up their deep-rooted feelings of weakness resulting from their fragile sense of self. Jobs and relationships that will make them feel like they are in charge and put them in a position of power are what they are often after. They love high-position jobs so that they can force others to do the things they want with their position and influence without it looking wrong. Their continual need for self-importance makes them seek positions of influence.

Unfortunately, they may also go all out to seek partners who are known for their strength just to enjoy the challenge of breaking them down with their acts.

Resents and Envies the Success of Others

When others accomplish something extraordinary, a narcissist may feel competitive towards them and see it as a threat to their superiority. Because they see others as competition, it makes them childish and envious of them. Because of the way they think, they also believe that other people are jealous of them.

Moody and Aggressive

Individuals tend to behave in predictable patterns of unpredictability when they have immature emotional development. They have an unstable behavior. They are whiny; they enjoy lashing out and often get busy plotting their revenge whenever they see themselves as a victim of someone's actions.

With all of these happening, your inner voice screams in your head, what is wrong with my spouse?

Defensive and Hypersensitive

You know you are dealing with an undeniably toxic person when they get annoyed so fast and fly into a rage whenever you disagree with anything they say. Every feedback you give them is seen as insulting or threatening. Any suggestion made to a narcissist that is contrary to what they have in mind is simply unwelcome.

Overinflated Sense of Entitlement

Narcissists have an overinflated sense of entitlement if they demand unquestioning and automatic compliance. They are people who act as if people owe them something special.

Sense of Entitlement Complex

When we threw tantrums as kids, not getting whatever we asked for, it looked cute. People would carry us and hold us in their arms, sweetly assuring us that we would receive what we wanted later, or we should only wait a little while, and we'd get it. They would gently wipe the tears away from our eyes and allow us to go and play.

As we became older, we started learning that we have to be patient and wait for our turn. We learnt that we have to be considerate and think of other people's needs and not only ours. Even though we may have learnt to show consideration for others, some people didn't.

They continued their habit of throwing tantrums into their adulthood, and tantrums were thrown in more mature and sophisticated ways. They continued to demand whatever they wanted from others and expected to be treated specially. If they didn't get it, they threw tantrums, but this time, not by rolling on the floor crying. They did it more subtly. They just feel that it is what they deserve, and they should be given special treatment.

Our parents and the society constantly tells us that we are unique and special beings, so having a sense of entitlement can easily be mistaken as natural, and even healthy.

Having a sense of entitlement can harm the people around us as it is self-love taken to the extreme. When we believe that we are the center of the universe, and the universe doesn't give us the particular thing we desire, all hell will break loose because we have already established a sense of entitlement.

Narcissists have the sense of entitlement trait, and this mindset is often developed as a result of failing to learn as children and young adults that other people don't exist just to meet our needs. For them, life is always all about them.

Let us break it down further by discussing the signs of a sense of entitlement complex.

Sense of Entitlement Symptoms

Narcissists exhibit a certain level of selfishness that makes other people's lives hard.

The symptoms of a sense of entitlement that narcissists exhibit include the following:

- They impose unrealistic demands on their spouse and those around them.

- They resort to self-pity when things don't go the way they planned and openly advertise this in melodramatic, attention-seeking ways.

- People have continuously called them a liar, bully, ruthless, manipulative, or an egotistical person.

- They go to extreme lengths to ensure their own happiness at the expense of others.

- They punish people with silent treatment, verbal or physical abuse when they don't do want they want.

- They see others as threats or competition to them, and they can go to any length to succeed.

- They exhibit many double-standards in their interactions with others. For example, they can do a particular thing, but you can't.

- They take more than they give in their relationships with others.

- They find it difficult to negotiate or reach a compromise because everything must be on their own terms.

- They have a conviction that they must always come first, even at the expense of others.

- They always get people upset by their actions and what they say.

- They like to assert their dominance or superiority over people and expect respect, admiration, and adoration from them because they think that they are better and more important.

Mind-Controlled by a Narcissist

Your self-esteem, health, and brain are in danger when you have a narcissist in your life. Controlling is just a part of the game they enjoy playing because they care about nothing but themselves.

Even though they are attracted to intelligent and confident people, they also break down intelligent and confident people.

Mind Control

Mind control is brainwashing or manipulative tactics done to take over a person's mind, which in turn affects the person's behavior.

Narcissists are skilled at using mind control on their victims. Coercive persuasion is a big part of mind control. Different techniques are used to manipulate someone to do what they want, and the victim is put under extreme stress and anxiety.

Subtle Control

Narcissists use subtle control, and you won't even know that you are doing exactly what they want you to do for them. They can use trigger phrases which include disappointment relating to their feelings, or even reminding you of how you should behave.

Narcissists are good at hiding their real nature. They will use a variety of strategies to get you to think and act a certain way, and they really don't care about your feelings or the pain you go through. They can use the tactics of love and flattery to manipulate you, and later control you with anger and aggression.

You will be isolated from others while they manipulate you, as this makes it easier for them to get into your mind and control you. They will make you live in constant fear by creating uncertainty, confusion, and chaos so that you are not sure of what to expect; this gives them more control over you.

They get to decide everything about your life, and you can't even escape it. Shifting blame and gaslighting are some of the techniques narcissists use on their victims.

How to Escape Mind Control

Once a narcissist is controlling you, it is difficult to get away from it. You may even need outside intervention before you can get away from their grip. A trusted family friend or therapist can help you figure out how to escape.

Physical escape will not be enough in this case; you will need to escape communications such as phone calls or even text messages that are aimed at manipulating and controlling you.

The narcissist is capable of making your identity disappear when their desires overshadow you. Your ability to make decisions on your own can be affected when your self-esteem and confidence gets shattered.

It takes time to heal from the divorce after ending the relationship with a narcissist, so don't jump right into another relationship. Take your time and heal. There are cases where people find themselves falling into a relationship with another narcissist after escaping and ending the relationship with one. Be careful so that this sad pattern doesn't repeat in your life.

You may be astounded by their mind control tactics. They are so good at it that they can convince you and even make you doubt your own memory. One phrase from them can get you fulfilling their desires in a hurry, so it best that you learn how to deal with them effectively.

Warning Signs of Narcissistic Control Freaks

Some warning signs of controlling narcissists are:

They Think They Know Everything

Narcissists always know what is best for you. They will even make your life miserable if you don't do what they suggest. A narcissist spouse feels they know your life better than you, so they won't stop yelling at you, threatening you, and pointing out all your mistakes and flaws. To them, they are the better directors of your life. They are even capable of pushing you into self-doubt and self-bullying, and you end up doubting your own judgment and following theirs.

Their Excitement Is Contagious

When a narcissist is excited about something, whether it's a career, a new product, or activity, it is the best, and you should better jump on board and feel the same way about it.

They Think They Don't Have Anything To Learn

A narcissist could be a new employee or an intern at a place, but they will feel that they already know everything and don't need to learn anything from people who are already doing their jobs well at the place.

They could also be a manager who insists on doing things their own way, with no input from other staff members even if they are failing at what they are doing.

They Are More Important Than the Rest of the World

You don't want to make your opinions matter because you are afraid of upsetting them. Your whole life should be devoted to meeting their needs.

They make their topics the focus of all conversations, and they get hurt easily. Their desires for the things they want are the only things they care about, and they will control and bully you whenever they want.

Everyone Around Them Is a Pawn in Their Game

As long as you can help them, you will have value in their eyes. They are selfish, demanding, and arrogant, and they think they deserve to be waited on. When you refuse to be a pawn in their game, you become an enemy. Distancing yourself from them could make them take notice and strike back at you.

They Are Saints In Their Own Mind

Every reason a narcissist gives for hurtful actions is always correct and enough to justify whatever they do. They don't consider their jealousy, anger, or hatred as bad characteristics, and they will see you as evil or as someone who doesn't understand what they are doing if you don't accept their actions. Self-deluded narcissists are saints in their own minds, and you better agree with them, or else they will see you as their enemy.

They Always Rule

Narcissists know how everyone should act in the world and how the world should be. They can strike back whenever they want, but everyone must follow their rules. It is your fault if their words or actions hurt you. They are self-righteous. They can talk loud and long until you decide to get on their team. They prefer to dominate and rule over their partners than to form a real relationship.

Narcissists have all these characteristics and won't give them up.

Shifting Personality

It involves having a poorly formed sense of self, which is displayed by acting kind and then becoming cruel and then shifting opinions. It is the basis of a poorly formed sense of self and is usually displayed in behavior such as kindness, followed by cruelty and shifting opinions.

You know your partner's character deficit is extraordinary if you have been frustrated with their behavior of presenting themselves as having solid and true opinions, only to give contradicting opinion hours later.

The persona they choose for themselves is usually based on the situation at hand, the people around them, and the goal they are trying to achieve, and what they would benefit from the character they are transforming into at that time.

You are stuck in a toxic relationship and a victim of narcissistic abuse if your spouse is displaying any of the traits discussed above. Warning bells should already be going off in your head.

Listen to these warning bells and say no to being their victim. Your self-worth is being shattered into a million pieces, but your survival instinct is refusing to allow it to continue.

Do something about it before it gets too late.

CHAPTER THREE

Narcissistic Love Bombing and Hate Bombing

Narcissistic Love Bombing isn't always what it looks like; it always leads to Hate Bombing.

Narcissistic Love Bombing isn't always what it looks like; it always leads to Hate Bombing.

I'm sure you must have asked the classic question, "why can't you go back to the way things used to be in the early days of the relationship?"

If you married a narcissist, you must have been wondering why things have changed so much. Well, here is something for you to know. There was never a good time in the relationship. What you remember as the good times that were so joyful was actually a well-thought-out emotional manipulation to drag you into your narcissist's trap.

Love bombing is used by narcissists mainly during the beginning of relationships to break down your emotional defenses, get into your heart, and get you to trust them. They make you get used to them by showing you love and care.

If you had paid more attention, you would have identified love bombing at the start of the relationship before your narcissist locks your heart away.

Love bombing is dangerous, and here is why.

Love-bombing feels so good when you are in the middle of it, so you won't easily recognize it as a form of abuse. It can include fast-tracking intimacy, excessive adoration, giving of chocolates, flowers, and lavish gifts, extravagant gestures, displays of affection, lots of attention, and deep praise about your personality traits. It can also include unconditional support and understanding like you have never experienced, talking about future plans on a second date, and a barrage of doting text messages and emails. They do this until you finally let down your guard and trust them early in the relationship, believing that they are indeed as nice as they present themselves to be.

Love bombing is a mind game that makes you trust them early, thinking they have good intentions when they are actually manipulating you.

You believe everything is real, and you never think that they might be putting on an act just to deceive you and get you to trust them because you would never deceive someone that way.

On a first date, a narcissist can say and do things intended to fast track the relationship, and these gestures imply a level of commitment that doesn't match with the length of time you two have known each other.

And make no mistake about this because there is nothing "loving" about this properly calculated and manipulative affection. It isn't real love. It is a self-centered pursuit to acquire you for their ego needs. You are just a shiny new toy that has captured their attention, and they want to play with you.

It feels so good to be true, and it's like having the sun shine on only you for the duration of the act. Love bombers don't really know who you are yet, so how can they be in love with you?

Love bombing isn't a sincere, romantic gesture. It is different. At the beginning of a new relationship, both parties do beautiful things for each other, and it is a normal thing. They want to make their new partner happy and to feel special. However, love bombers are usually self-serving, and their acts aren't real.

There is nothing wrong with treating someone to a surprise trip if you have known each other long enough for that. If the intention is also to get to know each other better, there is nothing wrong with it.

Love bombers usually fake a genuine interest in someone to get what they want from the person. They manipulate the person using grand gestures so that they can get sex, money, or even access to important personalities.

Grand gestures that should occur a year into a relationship is likely to put a potential mate off if it occurs in the first month of dating the person.

Love bombing is a show of desperation. The victim may not be interested in the flattery or love bombing anymore, so they may start feeling pressured.

A healthy individual does not need to try to force an instant bond; they know that a real relationship takes time to build. They respect the other person's boundaries, and they are willing to give them time and space. If a new relationship starts to look like a romantic movie, then you should pay more attention to what is going on.

The Love bomber's End Game

Love bombers treat a new relationship the way a salesperson works at closing a deal. Just like the salesperson does everything possible to close the sale, love bombers do everything possible to win you over through their excessive show of love, affection, and attention, which ends as soon as they feel they have won you over.

They seem to be the ones doing the giving until you realize that you have really been the one doing the giving, and they have been using you for their own selfish gains all along.

The narcissist may punish you to regain control if they feel like their position of power is threatened whenever you speak your mind or make plans with friends and family, leaving them out of the plans.

Things you do to prove that you are human and can assert your independence, like not wanting something the narcissist picks out for you, can even lead to brooding silence or flashes of anger.

Love bombing is the first phase of a narcissistic relationship. Let us discuss more about the love bombing phase and three other phases of the relationship.

Love Bombing Phase

The first is the Love Bombing Phase. During the love bombing phase, the narcissist gets you addicted to the excessive attention and affection they shower on you.

Narcissists shower their potential victims with excessive praise, attentiveness, and admiration to make them see that they can be fantastic partners for them if they get married.

This emotional manipulation phase is also used to learn more about you; they get to know your likes and dislikes, and your hopes and aspirations.

They are gathering all this information about you because it will come in handy later once the devalue phase begins; this can be really devastating and it is called cognitive empathy.

The narcissist hides their true self from you during this phase, so that they can get you to trust them. If they showed you their true self, you would run and never look back. They hide their true self so that they can succeed in deceiving you to stay with them.

Narcissists don't even have identities; they shapeshift to win the attention and admiration of those closest to them. The emotional manipulation via the love bombing phase can last for weeks or even months if the narcissist believes the potential gain is worth waiting for.

Love bombing can be in many forms. The narcissist sets aside their short-term ego boost so that they can work to earn your trust and gain in the long-term. They are hoping for a huge payoff, so everything they do for you at this stage is considered an investment in their future.

Narcissistic Devalue Phase

The second is the Narcissistic Devalue Phase. Love bombing doesn't last forever. Once the narcissist has gotten what they want from you, they'll discard you fast. A once affectionate person suddenly changes into an unaffectionate and controlling person.

The narcissist's true personality doesn't show overnight. It will slowly crack through the love bombing covering. They start by testing the waters with some passive-aggressive responses and insults to see your reaction to them.

If you don't give them the opportunity to treat you like thrash and you stand up for yourself during this phase, they may even get angry and quit the relationship so that they can be portrayed as the victim while they go on to search for someone that will tolerate their narcissistic behavior.

They will see you as someone who isn't worth the effort because you demanded respect, or they may also likely go back to the love bombing phase and do their work at winning your heart and getting you hooked a little more.

They will also include snippets of narcissistic devalue until they are 100% sure that they have hooked you, and you won't leave them. They want to make you believe that they can leave you and get another partner that is better than you any time they want to.

The narcissistic devalue phase can even last as long as the love bombing phase lasted. It can take weeks or months because they have a strategy that they are following, and they know what they are doing. They won't show you their full-blown narcissistic abuse traits too soon. The devalue phase can be totally overwhelming, or it can be subtle and barely noticeable.

After the devaluing and insults, did it take long for you to come around? Did you call them out immediately after they embarrassed you in public, or did you let it slide? Did you fire back or keep quiet when they said your success at work wasn't even a big deal?

What the narcissist is doing is that they are showing you their abusive behavior little by little so that they can gauge your response to it to enable them to strategize better and nail down a future emotional manipulation plan.

The love bomber's victim may try desperately to get back in the love bomber's good graces during the periods of devaluation. Some victims even give up family, friends, hobbies, and even jobs and financial stability because they want to win back their love bomber's attention and affection.

Full Blown Hate Bombing Phase

The third is the Full Blown Hate Bombing Phase. Most narcissistic relationships end with this phase, and it can go on for weeks, moths, or years.

Deep narcissistic abuse occurs at this stage because you are now caught up in their trap. Most victims of narcissistic abuse are so blinded by the emotional manipulation of the love bombing phase that they don't see the red flags in time until they find themselves in this phase.

The narcissist knows how to get you hooked by switching between hurling abuses at you and love bombing you. They love bomb you when they see that you are about to put an end to the relationship. It is done strategically to take your memory back to the good times you have enjoyed in the relationship.

Narcissistic Discarding Phase

The fourth is the Narcissistic Discarding Phase. If a narcissist discards someone, it should be taken as a positive thing even though it feels extremely painful.

Discarding happens if they feel that they have found someone else that will be a new supply and take your place. They can also discard you partially and then resort to love bombing if they feel that they aren't done with you yet.

When they feel that you have become too much work for them and they can easily attach themselves to someone else who can be easily manipulated, they will quickly discard you.

Most narcissists will not just discard you completely. They will instead give you the silent treatment and leave you hanging for some time so that they can easily return to the relationship when they want to. If you get lucky enough and you are discarded by a narcissist, then be happy and maintain no contact. It is the best thing for you to do.

Love bombing doesn't last forever. It always leads to hate bombing. The narcissist reverts to love bombing once they reach the devalue or hate bombing phase in order to grab your attention and stop you from leaving. They start showing their character slowly because they are wise enough to know that you will leave and never look back if they oppress you all the time.

They shower you with love to make you believe they care about you and convince you that they want you to have the best life. They want you to have it in your mind that if you can just obey them and play by their rules, they will treat you right.

Since the love bombing phase is emotional manipulation and exploitation, it will always take a turn for the worst at some point.

Many movies may glorify relationships starting with obsessive behavior, but keep it in mind that if something looks too good to be true, it probably is. Healthy relationships don't start with obsessive behavior.

CHAPTER FOUR

The Exhausted Spouse

"If you are suffering so badly in the marriage, why don't you just leave?"

You must have been asked that question too many times. The truth is that you know you are in a toxic relationship, but you are finding it difficult to take a walk. Why don't you just leave the relationship?

Toxic narcissism looks pretty on the outside but ugly on the inside. Everything looks nearly perfect on the outside, and people who aren't aware of your problems see your relationship as a perfect one because they aren't aware of all that is happening behind closed doors. And you also want people to see that you're happy; you don't want them to know how ugly the inside is. Am I right?

If you are married to a narcissist, and you manage to discuss your problems with someone outside of the relationship, they must have asked you the "why don't you just leave?" question many times.

Your life is really complicated, but this is what concerned friends and family members don't know.

The Complicated Price of Loving a Narcissist

Mental exhaustion is already associated with loving a narcissist, so no one else is permitted to add more problems to your life.

The act of isolation in an attempt to stay sane becomes a normal thing for you, and you gradually start preferring to run and hide yourself instead of engaging with normal, happy people. Sometimes, you just want to be left alone.

Your narcissist's behavior will even make you feel more isolated. They will do everything within their power to make you withdraw and stay alone. They do this to make you completely dependent on them financially, physically, and emotionally.

Narcissists have charming qualities, and that charm prevented you from seeing the narcissism when you first met them. They had something really enticing about them. They perfectly matched your needs and wants, and you felt an irresistible attraction towards them. However, after you walked down the aisle, the fairy tale world you had seen disappeared, and it seemed like your life came to a halt the day you walked down the aisle.

Seeing that your spouse has changed makes you so desperate to return to the fairy tale world you have enjoyed with them. To achieve this, you started doing whatever they demanded. Their demands continued, and all that you did was never enough for them. It seemed like the more you fulfilled their demands, the more the demands skyrocketed.

Desperate to put an end to the exhaustion you are feeling, you start looking for another solution; this is when you start taking a closer look at your partner's behavior and discover they are narcissistic.

You are meant to meet their needs every single time. They even expect you to know when they need admiration and adoration. With them, it's a one-way street where you keep giving until you get exhausted, and they don't give you in return.

According to them, you are the one who is always needy, ungrateful, and never satisfied with everything they do for you. None of your friends and family members who have known you longer than your spouse have ever made any of such complaints about you. None has ever said you have unreasonable expectations of them, like your spouse accuses you of.

Your spouse gets jealous of anything that takes your attention away from them. You get blamed for the rage their jealousy triggers. People they can get jealous of because they think those people have your attention over them may include children, friends, or family. They can even get jealous over pets or your occupation.

When you get provoked by their cruelty, and you leave during an argument with them, two things happen:

It makes them know that you will one day leave them, and this sets them up to become the victim. Now, this is just ammunition they have gained to be used against you.

There is nothing unconditional about the love a narcissist gives. They punish you with neglect or abuse. They can abuse you physically, emotionally, sexually, financially or even psychologically. When it comes to neglect, they withhold their love, communication, attention and support.

A narcissist will threaten abandonment if you refuse to do what they want. Your fear of abandonment would make you unable to leave the marriage if you had abandonment issues before you married the narcissist. To keep you under their control, the abandonment issues you have could even be the reason why they targeted you for marriage in the first place.

Your narcissist partner will use remorse as a manipulation tool to get you to trust them again because they expect everything to return to normal speedily.

Trust was the basis of your relationship, but now you have no trust left to give to your partner. The game is over because you can't keep fighting and crying. You can't seem to understand who broke them so badly that they aren't able to feel consistently happy with anyone, even themselves. The beast inside them doesn't hesitate to tear you apart, feast on the vulnerabilities you entrusted to them, and spread the news about your incompetency around town.

Many spouses ignored the warning signs and went on to get themselves trapped in a marriage with the narcissist. Paying closer attention to these signs in the early days of your relationship could have saved you from the terrible situation you are now in, but you ignored them and still walked yourself into the ditch.

Despite everything they put you through with blood dripping down your face, your beautiful mask of happiness perfectly remains in place. You practice putting on a smile everywhere you go to hide the terrible pain you feel inside.

Naively, you hoped that putting enough effort into making the marriage work and communicating honestly and effectively would turn things around. You hoped that if you were kind enough, supportive enough, sexy enough, creative enough, and successful enough, things would become better in the marriage. You even thought about cutting ties with your friends and business partners that your partner didn't approve of, but it didn't change things.

Your partner shines a fake light on the public to strengthen their ego and help them gain more power, but they bring darkness to their own home and don't even care about it.

They tell you the qualities that you lack, and you try to work on them one after the other. Once you have developed yourself and fixed the issues they complained about, they change the rule to their game. All of a sudden, there is something new that is disappointing them; something you lack. It goes on and never ends. It is impossible for you to ever measure up or find stable ground, so the relationship is forever off-balance.

Your partner is addicted to the feeling of being in control. After several months or years of abuse, when you summon the courage to finally question their actions or express yourself, negative consequences follow.

You find it easier to sit in silence, rather than start a fun and peaceful conversation with them because it could anger the beast in them and turn the peaceful talk into an unwarranted rage.

Distorted versions of intimate secrets you entrusted to your spouse are shared with their friends and family and laughed about for maximum humiliation and over-the-top character assassinations.

Lies and exaggerated versions of stories are told in rooms full of people and even to your closest friends to increase the pain and loneliness the torture is causing you.

If you react and attempt to discuss your feelings, you will be called crazy. Your pain will be ignored and talked about like it is pointless to even bring it up.

Should their cruelty break you completely and make you scream and yell back in their face out of sheer frustration, suddenly that is what will become the topic for discussion; your behavior and never theirs.

Your behavior will become the topic they will use against you for all future fights. And even then, your reaction will be twisted from the reality and exaggerated to make them look like the victim so that you can apologize to them.

Once they have made you look like the devil, they come back as though nothing has happened and expect you to welcome them with open arms and a smiling face.

You will be too exhausted to restart the pain again by bringing up the issue that caused the fight. You just want everything to be swept under the rug and be so relieved that the punishment is over, until the next time.

You will lose so much of yourself and eventually stop fighting back once this starts happening to you all the time because ignoring and not fighting back is the only way you can get find temporary relief.

Narcissists install a mental filter in your head, and before you know what is happening, everything you say or do passes through this filter. "Will they get upset if I say or do this?" you start asking yourself questions like this before making any move. Your wants and desired are pushed aside and expressing your needs only leads to more pain, so you get conditioned to not having your needs met.

You are always tormented by the fear of their next outburst and their disgust for you for no reason. Your behavior was always the cause of their anger, so you constantly had to walk on eggshells.

Many times you have been too exhausted to even get out of bed. Your heart skips in fear every time they call out to you. Your sense of self becomes non-existent, and you feel like there is nothing left to live for.

Narcissistic abuse is domestic violence creeping in slowly until everything gets out of hand, and you become completely unrecognizable.

It takes time, dedication, and work to recover from this kind of abuse. You love your partner when they are kind. You also love the idea of them being peaceful, but you don't know when that will happen.

It can be embarrassing for you to admit some of the things you go through in your home, but realize that narcissists are pathological. You could set a watch by their behaviors because they are entirely predictable. Once you learn the games they play, you will understand their predictability.

After all that you have been through in the marriage, you finally come to a point when you decide not to play their game any longer. You don't believe the tearful stories they tell of remorse and self-reflection because you don't see any changes in them.

Sometimes, you ignore their texts, emails, apologies, and declarations of love, and sometimes, you yearn to hear from them because you badly want to believe them.

You must realize that you don't owe them anything. Learn to give yourself the love you worked so hard to win from someone who has no love to give.

Freedom begins with you facing reality, admitting the truth of who they are, accepting your responsibilities, and moving on with your life.

CHAPTER FIVE

Divorcing a Narcissist: The Utter Hell

Being married to a narcissist is hard, but divorcing a narcissist is even harder. Some people start and never finish the divorce process; fear, intimidation, and exhaustion keep them back from making it to the end.

Your partner will be happy seeing you down and battling with the process because they thrive on seeing you suffer for daring to stand up to them.

If you find yourself in the terrible position of ending a marriage with a narcissist, you must realize that you need to be courageous because it isn't a fight for the faint of heart. You must buckle up and get yourself prepared for the long, nasty ride.

Spouses of narcissists know that their partner can make them believe that the sky has been red all along, and make it look like they have been crazy to think otherwise. They are that good at making you feel like you are the crazy one, and they could never be wrong about anything.

The Ultimate Ego Bruiser

The period of divorce is a horrible time for anyone going to the court, having to meet up with lawyers, and having money talks. If the marriage has children, you will also have a frustrating experience dividing time spent with the children.

Emotional distress is inescapable during this time because you are putting an end to a relationship with someone that you once loved. It hurts a lot because they used to be madly in love with you, or appeared to be, but now they are madly in love with themselves. The divorce process itself involves legal jargons, structure, and rigidity that can make you sick.

Only the narcissist wins in a divorce because they have no empathy. People with empathy are aware that nobody wins in a divorce. Divorce changes everything about your life. Your daily routine, your home; your life basically flips inside out. Even divorce that was peacefully done still brings hurt and pain.

Even if you approach them politely, the narcissist sees any threat to their self-esteem as a personal attack. They believe that divorce is a sign of weakness and failure. For them, it is the ultimate ego Bruiser.

After the divorce papers have been filed, it becomes a game of who should win the divorce. Their every move is calculated because they want to win. It is a game to them, and they are the only one to decide when it is over. They can raise hell at even the littlest of things

When their self-image is at stake, they can do anything to play the deceptive part of being the injured party. They have no shame and feel no remorse for their actions, so nothing is off-limits for them to do. Even if they have to expose your private information and details of your life to give the impression that you are an incapable parent, they will do it. If they were to be the judge of the case, you would have no rights as a parent or even a human being.

No Fan of Peace

Narcissists always have a goal to win, even if they make it look like peace is all they want.

Money is insignificant to narcissists. Talking about money, they will empty your bank account and drain you completely, and once they are finished, they will move over to friends and family to continue exploiting them. The narcissist isn't a fan of peace.

Before you know it, you will have wasted so much money fighting over something not really significant. And it won't stop there. It will continue.

All the energy you have left will be drained from your body; they will portray you as a monster and a complete piece of shit. The failure of the marriage and the divorce just has to be your fault. Your narcissist will find a way to make you carry the blame.

Narcissists will twist every single thing you do and make you look like who you are not, just to make people see you as a monster. They never surrender without completely destroying their victim.

They have an explanation for everything, and the death of your sanity doesn't even matter to them. All that matters is for them to win at the end. They have a well thought out explanation for the wrong things that happened to them, and it excludes them being the reason for any of the wrongs. They will never take the blame. It will never be because of their inappropriate behavior; it will be because the judge was unfair, or the lawyer was incapable, or the court system was simply unjust. They are even ready to take all their loved ones down with them.

After you fight the battle of divorce, winning would be the last thing on your mind because your aim was just to get out of the hell you have living in. Your narcissist spouse would have been reminding you all along that you don't deserve to win so, winning this psychological war means nothing to you because you will have already made yourself believe that you don't deserve it.

And this isn't the last you would hear of them. Know that your narcissist will tell their story to everyone who cares to listen, even long after the divorce is over. They are excellent liars and manipulators so be prepared to hear them telling people manipulative stories and spreading lies about you just to gain their sympathy or praise.

You may document interactions with your narcissist spouse because lies and deceit are a part of them. It may be absurd, but that is the reality you now live in. You must do this because no one will even believe you when you tell them things your partner does, and your partner has also succeeded in convincing you that you are crazy, so this documentation is necessary for you to do.

When you're trying to talk to someone who doesn't reason with logic, you'll be wasting your time. You keep showing them how the situation isn't right, but your words are only falling on deaf ears, and all of your efforts are useless. It may look like you have given up on happiness, but the truth of the matter is that you're just trying to stay sane.

Being the straight-thinking one in the marriage, and trying to keep quiet, while your partner makes your life a living hell, can be more complicated than the divorce itself.

As they try to push you over the edge on purpose so that their actions can be justified, they will also pile up evidence to back up the picture of the person they have painted you to be.

Narcissists function with havoc. Chaos gives them energy. While you long for the chaos to come to an end so that things can finally become normal again, it will never be normal again. The unfortunate truth is that narcissists thrive in chaos, and they can't exist without it. If a situation they have with someone gets resolved and things become okay, they seek out someone else to disrupt and control; this is their lifestyle, and they thrive on it.

Divorce isn't pretty. It is terrible. Nobody gets married thinking about divorce right from the beginning of the marriage. They never plan to divorce one day until it happens, so divorce comes with its own hurt and pain. Divorcing a narcissist is worse than the pain and hurt associated with a normal divorce, it is humiliating and exhausting.

Since they are so in love with themselves, they carry their loved ones through their own ruins without minding the cost.

Even though divorcing your narcissist partner can make your whole year the worst you ever lived, it would still be the best decision for you to make and you would definitely do it all over again after going through the experience they have put you through.

Rules When Divorcing a Narcissist

It doesn't matter how long you have been married for, whether it's been four days or forty years, you find it difficult to believe that you are now divorcing the person you pledged your life and undying love to. Many couples getting divorced have said that the very traits that made them fall in love with their partner are the very traits causing them to fall out of love with them.

Divorcing a narcissist is hell on earth. Narcissists appear to be in love with themselves, but contrary to what it seems, they have very fragile self-esteem hidden behind their confidence and grandeur. They are afraid of been seen as imperfect, so they make themselves appear perfect.

They are highly sensitive to criticism because of the fragile nature of their self-esteem. They find it difficult regulating their emotions and reactions to situations.

The thought of looking anything less than perfect traumatizes a narcissist; that is why they do everything within their power to make their partner look like the bad guy. Only a raging 2-year-old can understand why they need to win.

Narcissists refuse to play by the normal divorce rules, so divorcing them is usually an ugly, exhausting and expensive business.

The legal drama, the financial issues and the emotional issues associated with divorce make it a complicated process, but with your partner being a narcissist, it can be more complicated. It can be a long, drawn-out process.

There are some steps you can take to divorce them on your terms, and not theirs. Let us discuss the steps.

Find Out If Your Partner Is Really a Narcissist

Your partner may have some character issues like being mean-spirited, arrogant or an egomaniac, but it doesn't make them a narcissist.

Narcissists are known for not taking any blame and for having no empathy at all. They won't feel any remorse or feel sorry for running over someone's puppy. They might even be blaming the puppy for crossing the road or getting angry with the owner of the puppy for having to clean their own blood-stained tires caused by the death of the puppy. Narcissists can be like that with no empathy at all.

Now imagine what will happen if you ask such a person who thinks so highly of themself for a divorce.

Will they even care about what they have to you to lead you to this decision? They probably won't think they have done anything to warrant a divorce. Are they also going to co-parent the children with you and protect them against the insecurities and uncertainties of life? They probably won't do that.

Even if you are getting a divorce because they were cheating on you, they will never take the blame; they will still blame you for being the reason for their cheating habits. If they also hit you physically or emotionally assaulted you, you also made them do it. It's all your fault. They will play the victim and go all out to punish you just to make you pay.

Dealing with a narcissist during a divorce is not an easy thing to do. They will be extraordinarily difficult to deal with, so you must put your guard up and be ready to face their troubles. Go all out to kill them with kindness, but they will still come after you. That is just who they are.

Rational Thoughts Should Be Reserved for the Right Audience

Narcissists don't value rational thoughts. Bringing rational thoughts while having a conversation with them won't be effective. It is just like a mother force-feeding her child who keeps spitting the food out. If the child wants ice-cream, they will cry and throw tantrums until you give them ice-cream. A narcissist is just that way; they will throw tantrums to get what they want. They must win at all costs. Everyone has to know that they were the one doing the right thing in the relationship. They want that vindication from the world. They throw tantrums to distract you and keep you off balance.

You can say something like, "I want primary custody of the kids because you often get drunk on alcohol." The narcissist will respond to you with "I can't trust you to properly care for our kids because you had a sexual affair with our son's soccer coach." You spend time explaining to them that you never even met your son's soccer coach and what they are accusing you of doesn't even have anything to do with your parenting ability.

The thing is, you have already taken the bait and discussing the topic your partner has chosen to talk about. Their preferred topic of discussion is your inability to parent while yours is their ability to parent.

Don't keep arguing with your partner. Just leave them alone and speak calmly and rationally to your lawyer about it. They will understand your rational thoughts, so let them speak to your narcissist partner on your behalf.

Get a Divorce Attorney That Specializes in Narcissism Cases

Know that your divorce will not be amicable. People married to narcissists often make the mistake of underestimating how terribly frustrating their divorce is probably going to be.

Couples reason together and try to work things out and do things amicably. That is definitely a great strategy if you are married to a normal person, but not to a narcissist. When you are married to a narcissist, it is an entirely different game. Your niceness only leads to them taken advantage of you in an epic way.

"Lawyering up" may not sound to you like the best thing to do, but it is best for you to get good legal advice before you can get started with the divorce process. You don't have to hire a physical warrior who will draw the battle line, but you do need someone strong at heart that can stand by your side throughout the period of the divorce.

When you are divorcing a bully, you need to hire a strong, but reasonable, divorce lawyer who isn't afraid to represent you against your bully. Don't get someone who will fight physically, though. The lawyer you hire shouldn't be someone who thrives on drama because narcissists also thrive on drama. If you hire this type of lawyer to represent you, you will only end up creating excess drama in your divorce. The best you can do is to find a fighter who won't actually fight physically; someone who will protect you from your narcissist partner, but not someone who will make your case worse than it already is.

Not all divorce attorneys are equal. Some have excellent negotiating skills, some are great talkers, and some aggressive. Understand this when you are trying to hire a divorce attorney that will help you with your divorce. You should seek out someone who understands the tactics that narcissists use in court. Get someone with experience in divorce cases like yours. They will be able to create a strategy that will help you through the legal process, thereby giving you a smooth ride through the divorce and custody proceedings.

Know What Is Ahead

Your narcissist ex will try to convince people that they're a better parent to the children; this will give you a hard time as you will have to convince different people that you are the parent best equipped to take care of the children properly.

You will have audiences, including judges, therapists, or counselors, and the narcissist will try to convince them that you're incompetent to raise the kids.

Your narcissist ex will be watching you closely to see if you will react emotionally to the accusations they are making against you. If you do, then you're acting out the part of the person they have manufactured for you thereby following their plan.

Divorcing them won't come that easy without them putting up a fight, so expect the unexpected and worst behavior from them during this period. You can't be knocked off balance.

Document

An ex can easily edit an email, text message or voice mail you have sent them before sending it off to their attorney. They can do this to create evidence to be used against you.

Be prepared for this. You can counter their claims against you if you have the original messages saved somewhere. You can provide the original message to prove your innocence. You can send screenshots of your conversations and audio recordings of your communications with your ex.

Try to keep track of all your conversations with your ex and avoid reacting to their provocative behaviors. Don't get into a fight or an argument with them at the PTA meeting either; others will be watching, and it can count as evidence to be used against you in court.

Also, save any proofs of their aggressiveness, bad behaviors, or abuse displayed on social media before they delete such posts. It can help you in court.

Create a Plan and Follow It

You have created a plan that you want to follow. It involves dividing all your assets reasonably so that you and your children will have no issues with moving on with your lives.

Ensure that you include as little time as possible to have contact with your ex after the divorce, even if your children have to spend some time with your ex. Your ex being a narcissist doesn't stop the children from spending some time with them.

Your ex won't see things the way you do. For them, it's about losing or winning. They want everything to themselves and nothing for you. They will do anything possible to keep you from achieving your goals and will spend any amount of money needed to accomplish that. They can spend $50k in legal fees just to keep you from getting a $25k property. Even if the judge gives you the right to the property, your narcissist ex would have something to talk about for the rest of his life. He will say the judge was unfair to him and that in itself is a win for your ex.

When you make your plan, know what you are willing to give up during the sharing of assets and responsibilities. You can demand an equal division of everything when you are discussing so that your ex is happy that they denied you something you really wanted to keep when any rational person would have easily given that up from the first day.

Circle the Wagons

Don't battle your ex alone. Before you divorce, you should assemble your support team. Surround yourself with your close friends, family members, and counselors at this time. Unite with them and stay protected.

Narcissists can spread lies about you to tarnish your image and ruin your relationship with people forever. They enjoy getting people to show them support, so they will do their best to paint you as the bad guy. They will even try to get to your family and friends before you if they can so they can tell them lies about you.

You can't stop your narcissistic spouse from gathering people and talking thrash about you to them, but you can have your close support group who already knows the truth about the situation so they can stand by you during this period.

By circling the wagons and fighting from all sides, a caravan could have all members defended against attack. Expect to be attacked from all angles when you are divorcing a narcissist. You won't be battling alone if you get yourself surrounded by your loved ones.

Get Yourself a Therapist

Narcissistic behavior can make you go crazy. A therapist will help you calm your nerves when all hell breaks loose. Your sanity will be preserved as they will act as your reality-check during your divorce process.

Getting yourself a therapist who has experience in dealing with narcissists can also guide you on the best strategies you can use during your divorce.

Ensure You Get Everything in Writing

Narcissists will say one thing today and then say another thing tomorrow. Lying comes naturally to them. They will never accept that they changed the story they told you previously, and you will even start thinking you are wrong and believing they are right because they will be so convincing about it.

The only way you can document everything that is happening is to get it in writing. You will need to use the emails and texts in court as evidence. Emails written by your spouse will be more convincing than the one you wrote.

If your partner fixes the time to pick the kids from school at 3 pm and they later lie and claim they said 7 pm, you will have the email from them to present as evidence of the lie.

Stay Out of Court as Much as You Can

Courtrooms are made for drama, and that is what narcissists are known for. They thrive on drama. Continually going to court adds more fuel to the fire in your divorce. Your narcissistic partner will also do really well in court if they are charming, attractive, and intelligent. They will do really well in court at first before the judge gets to understand who they are. Your partner succeeded in charming you when you first met them, so be aware that they can also charm the judge too.

Your partner's true colors will only begin to show after many court appearances. Their true colors may never be seen in court if they can act really well. The whole divorce process will be completed without anyone in court, even noticing their true character. Because of their charming behavior, the judge might even be thinking that you are the one who is crazy.

That is why it is a good thing to use mediation or Collaborative Divorce when divorcing your narcissistic partner.

Make Your Narcissistic Spouse "Win"

If you want to get through your divorce with your sanity still intact, make your narcissistic spouse win. It sounds crazy, but it is a great strategy. It works because narcissists love to win. So, if you can find more ways to make them look good and feel like they have won, you will definitely increase your chances of going through your divorce process fast.

Find ways to make them win without losing the things that are truly of great importance to you; this is a great strategy to use if you can do it right.

Pick Your Battles Wisely

Get ready to fight a lot of battles after you divorce your narcissist spouse. You have to pick your battles wisely so that you don't end up broke and exhausted because you are fighting every battle that comes your way.

You will have drained your energy with unimportant battles and already be exhausted when the battles you care about the most come around. To avoid losing the battles you care about, it is wise that you pick your battles wisely.

To ensure that you don't fight every single fight your narcissistic partner drags you into; you need to make your plan in advance and decide which battles are worth your time and effort and which ones you must ignore and let go.

Walk away from the fights that don't matter, and you will be saving yourself some precious time, energy, and resources.

You will also succeed in leaving your spouse wondering why you aren't fighting all the battles they are bringing your way and what you are up to.

Set Boundaries and Stick to Them

Setting healthy boundaries where partners respect each other's opinions help in building healthy relationships. Narcissists don't respect boundaries and don't even notice their partner's needs.

Since you were not used to setting boundaries during your marriage to your narcissistic spouse, setting them during your divorce can be challenging for you.

Now that you have made up your mind to divorce your spouse, it is crucial that you set clear boundaries about what kind of treatment you will tolerate and what you won't put up with from now on.

You need to do this because it will help you start having some quality time to yourself so you can separate from your spouse. If you will still be seeing your spouse because you will be co-parenting together, setting boundaries will help you set the tone of your post-divorce relationship.

Forgive Yourself

You may be unable to forgive yourself for getting married to a narcissist. It is hard for you to imagine why you let it happen. Well, there is nothing you can do now to erase the past, so forgive yourself.

Since narcissists like to win at all costs, you were the prize while you both were dating, so they did all they could to win you. They put on their charm and brought their A-game to make you theirs. Their confident, can-do-all, always-close-the-sale, and charming attitude may be what even won your heart in the first place.

After they have won you as their price, you start seeing the changes in them as they shift their attention to the next price to be won. It could be pursuing a promotion at work or some other achievement they hold in high esteem. This coldness in their behavior will make you start the divorce process.

Don't get worked up about it because you didn't see it coming. You have learnt something valuable from the marriage. At least you now know the narcissistic behaviors to look out for if you ever want to find yourself a new partner.

Take Good Care of Yourself

You need to take good care of yourself if you want to make it to the end. Don't go thinking that divorce is a sprint; it isn't; it is a marathon; this is especially true when the spouse you are divorcing is a narcissist. It is more like an ultra-marathon when divorcing a narcissist.

Don't get yourself stressed out. Ensure that you are eating well, having a good night's sleep, and exercising regularly. Create time to do the things you love so that you can laugh and be happy. It will help lighten the burden of divorce for you.

Having a solid support group and a therapist to lean on will help you reduce your loneliness and isolation during this period.

CHAPTER SIX

Mind Games Narcissists Play

You need to be prepared to face the worst when divorcing a narcissist. Divorcing them can create a level of agony that is too difficult to bear.

One of the biggest issues you will face when divorcing a narcissist is that you will almost get played for a fool, so be prepared for that. You expect your narcissistic partner to be as reasonable as you so your divorce can be amicable, but you get slammed.

Before your narcissistic partner's power-play turns you into a shadow of yourself, it's best to understand the mind games narcissists play. Understanding this will help you survive when you are divorcing them.

Here are some mind games that narcissists play:

The Blame Game

We know that narcissists won't accept responsibility for any negative thing that happens. To them, everything that has led to the failure of the marriage is your fault. Even if you caught them cheating on you many times, they would still say it wasn't their fault.

As you keep trying to prove that you are right, they will also double their efforts at proving you are wrong.

Snake Charming

Narcissists present themselves well in court since many of them are very accomplished and highly driven professionals. Everyone will find them amazingly charming, and this will make the divorce process more difficult for you. Their charming behavior can put you at a disadvantage until the judge finally realizes that your narcissistic spouse may not be as amazingly wonderful as they appear to be.

Make You Look Crazy

Narcissists can just walk into your home and carry the kids away without your notice. They don't respect boundaries. They can do just about anything they want with their parenting time, and this includes dropping the kids off too early or showing up late.

They will just assume that you will be there when they are not. When you get divorced, your narcissistic ex will walk all over you unless you set firm boundaries in writing and enforce them.

Narcissists will deliberately say and do things that will make you look crazy. When you run to the court to report the issue, your ex will deny ever saying or doing such. Everyone will then look at you like you are the one who is crazy.

Truth or Dare

If you think a narcissist will tell the truth in court just because they swore to tell the truth, then you are mistaken. They won't, because to them, "truth" is relative. They are ready to say and do just about anything that will make people see them as the good person and see you as the bad one. If you believe that they will tell the truth, to your utmost surprise, they will walk all over you in court, and you will be left standing in court with your mouth wide gaping open watching them lie to the judge and the judge nods their head in approval, believing every word they say.

My Way or the Highway

We know that narcissists can never be wrong. They are so quick to paint you as a fool or explode in anger if you ever choose your way over theirs. They are quick to judge, criticize, and ridicule you, but will accuse you of abusing them if you try to do the same thing to them.

For them, it's "my way or the highway".

Master at Convincing

Narcissists are masters at convincing you that they have changed, and this makes it difficult to deal with them. They can suddenly turn around and treat you with kindness and concern after troubling you so much and making you go crazy. As soon as you forget about the pain they have caused you and you forgive them thinking they have truly changed for the better, they strike and take advantage of you.

What Rules?

The narcissist thinks that rules don't apply to them, so they never follow the rules. They won't respect a court order that they don't agree with. They won't stick to a parenting schedule or even pay support. They will do things they are not supposed to do, and you won't get any reasonable answer from them when you ask them about it. They will have excuses to justify their actions and even deny violating the court order.

Shapeshifting

To get attention and sympathy, your narcissist ex can quickly morph into whatever form they choose. They will become weak when you are strong and make themselves appear like they are the victim of your abuse. They will also not hesitate to paint you as incompetent and lazy if you are weak. The most frustrating thing is that they will change as soon as you change yourself; you can't succeed in pinning them down even if you tried.

Hide and Seek

Narcissists project the negative traits that they have onto others because they have fragile egos. Deep within, they feel less than perfect, but they never admit it even to themselves. After divorcing them, they will accuse you of everything they are doing, such as lying or manipulating the kids.

The Drama Dance

Drama puts narcissists in the spotlight, so they love it. Since they enjoy spreading negative emotions, drama puts them in the spotlight and gives them the feeling of power. Because they love drama, going to court with them is disastrous as they will turn the courtroom into their playground and put on their best act. So, you're simply deluding yourself if you think divorcing your narcissist partner will be easy or amicable because it won't. Be prepared for the drama.

Winner Takes All

Since divorce is a game to narcissists, they have to win. They don't mind you losing every penny you have as long as they are winning. Your children's lives may be on the verge of being destroyed if they win, but they may also be okay with that. Their "winner takes all" attitude makes them not to be concerned about the consequences of their win. It is extremely difficult to reach a reasonable settlement with a narcissist during a divorce process.

You can survive the divorce with a narcissist, so you don't have to get yourself worked up over your partner's troubles.

Every divorce comes with pain, and you can expect yours to be toxic if your spouse is a full-blown narcissist. You may not be able to change your spouse or to tame them, but you can take steps to protect yourself and your children from trauma.

Tactics Narcissists Use On Their Spouse

Divorcing a narcissist can feel impossible. As the divorce progresses, more insane things will begin to happen. You can witness your spouse transform from yelling at you in the car on your way to an event to becoming the most charming person in the room when you get to the event you are going to. During your marriage, you will get used to their radical changes in personality, depending on who was or wasn't in the room.

You will feel puzzled, scared, numb, responsible, and disorganized by their behavior after the divorce papers have been filed. They will be the victim in front of the family members, but when you are alone with them, they will threaten you. They will become amazingly charismatic and then beg you again.

The surprising abusive attacks following their desperate pleas to remain together can leave you confused and frustrated.

They are capable of charming friends, lawyers, and even judges into believing that they are the victims, leaving the real victim without any support.

Here are a few of the tactics used by narcissists.

Bait and Switch

A narcissist will attempt to lure you into their way of perceiving the world by dangling attractive bait like money or success. The bait will then be used against you when you, the victim, least expect it. They can turn around and say you only married them for the money.

- **Accusations = Secrets**

  This method is the defense mechanism of projection where the narcissist accuses you of improper behavior such as adultery. In this case, the narcissist who accuses you of adultery is with the adultery secret.

- **Blowups = Diversion**

  During a divorce, your spouse can rant for no real reason just to divert attention from the issue at hand. It is just like complaining about a lite candle when the whole house is actually burning down.

- **Gifting = Attention**

  Your spouse can give you an expensive and unnecessarily extravagant gift to try and increase your responsiveness. A narcissist doesn't give a free gift. Gifts like these are usually given to gain your attention or favor.

- **Innocent Delays = Guilty Actions**

  Narcissists use tactics like excessive motions, delaying hearings, and dragging out meditations to cover up their guilty actions so that you can give in to them.

Scare Tactics

Narcissists use abusive scare tactics and can threaten to harm you regardless of how you feel. They act like the bully who often intimidates other children into giving them their lunch money.

- **Alienation**

  One of the ways your spouse gets you to comply is to alienate you from your friends and family because they are more likely to make you feel alone and abandoned until you give in to their demands.

- **Silent Treatment**

Another simple tactic your spouse can use to intimidate you is to refuse to speak to you at all. Once they start giving you the silent treatment, they will make you eventually give in to their demands just because you want to break the tension. The person that speaks first is the one who loses.

- **Recreating Historical Events**

This is a more advanced method where your spouse mixes a bit of truth with a lot of fiction to make you believe that your perception of the event is the inaccurate version. Personal historical events are recreated to make them look like the sane one while you look like the insane one.

- **Verbal Assaults**

When your spouse has tried different tactics, and they all fail, they will resort to making subtle verbal threats in an attempt to terrorize you. Unfortunately, they can be clever enough not to put it in writing so that they go undetected by others and leave you with no proof.

Rollercoaster Ride

When you are divorcing a narcissist, the ups, downs, twists, turns, and surprises of a rollercoaster ride happen. Since it is all about control for a narcissist, they remain in control by generating an air of uncertainty.

- **I Love You / I Hate You**

  The narcissist can bring this twist to appeal to your emotional side. They can remind you of their love at one time to generate feelings of nostalgia, and they can say, "I hate you" to intentionally hurt you.

- **They Say You Can Have It All / They Mean You Can Have Nothing**

  Your spouse may want to play the victim, so in an attempt to do that, they will claim that you can have everything. But they will secretly tell their attorney that they won't give you anything.

- **They Say They Want This To Be Over / They Mean It's Never Going To Be Over**

  In the presence of the attorney, mediator, judge, family members, and friends, your spouse can claim that they want this to be over. But in reality, they don't want it to be over. They will find ways to have control over you even after the divorce is over, and you are trying to move on with your life.

- **They Say You Will Never See Me Again / They Mean You Are Always Going To Be Mine**

   Your spouse can threaten to abandon you to make you say that you want them to remain in your life. Once that is communicated, they will begin to say that you will always be theirs, even after divorce.

Child's Play

Divorcing a narcissist can have negative a negative impact on the children. When both parents are still together, you are always available to provide attachment and empathy. However, as the children grow older, they may begin to think that narcissistic behavior is acceptable, and they may not fully understand the effects of narcissism.

- **Disney Parenting**

   After the custody is settled, your spouse can become the Disney parent. They start acting all fun and exciting around the children and making them believe that there will never be a dull moment when they are with them, and rules can be broken too. They do all these just to lure the children away from you.

- **Parental Alienation**

Next, your spouse begins to alienate your children from you by pointing out the hurt they have experienced in your hands. They start talking to the children about the inconsistencies they have been through and pointing out your flaws to make them shy away from you in favor of them.

- **Picking Favorites**

Your spouse will single out any child who does not conform as disrespectful, irresponsible, ungrateful, and rebellious. They will then shower the other children with gifts, attention, and praises. This act of theirs can give rise to conflict amongst the siblings.

- **Custody Threat**

Your spouse will make threats of changing the custody arrangement whenever you don't agree with them or their parenting. They sometimes carry out this threat not because they really want to spend more time with the children but because they want to hurt you.

Once you become aware of these tactics, you will no longer be shocked by your ex's behavior. You will start thinking more clearly and be able to make the best decisions for you and your children's future.

Resisting Mind Games When Divorcing a Narcissist

When divorcing your narcissistic partner, it is advisable that you do the following to help you tackle the mind games they play.

Keep All the Important Papers

Make sure you collect all the important papers. Keep birth certificates, marriage certificate, copies of bills, and all the papers that are necessary for the divorce because if you ever get into a situation where you need anything from your ex, be sure that they will not give it to you. They will lie that they don't have it, they will give you some lame excuse, or simply say no that they won't give it to you.

Be Smart

You have to think fast when dealing with a narcissist and be very smart because if you choose to play it cool, you are going to get yourself into stress. So, it's better for you to use everything you have against them.

Remember that they can present themselves as perfect humans through their devious actions that will make the judge believe their side of the story, so be prepared for that. To prevent this from ruining you, use all means possible to make the judge see how cunning they really are.

Don't Fall Into Traps

Your ex is devious enough to use all your frustration outbursts against you. They will be watching for outbursts from you, so ensure that you cease all unnecessary communication with them. They will deliberately provoke you to make you angry so that you can say awful things to them via phone calls that they will record, or send messages that they can use against you.

Ensure that you suppress your anger, or express it elsewhere. Don't allow yourself to get manipulated. If you do, you will be allowing yourself to fall freely into the trap they have set for you.

Maintain your no contact rule with them; don't break it. If you do, they will make use of that opportunity to manipulate you and make you pay for everything they think you have done to them.

Get Your Children the Help They Need

Children are usually victims in the case of a divorce between a narcissist parent and a normal parent because the narcissist parent will stop at nothing. They will easily harm the children without feeling any remorse for their actions if it will hurt you because they only have their own interests at heart.

Your kids may be quiet about the divorce and may not say anything about it to you, but that doesn't mean they are okay. They may be bottling up their feelings and hurting badly inside. It is okay for you to hire a counselor that can talk to the children and help them open up and deal with the divorce better.

The Harassment Will Continue

Know that your ex won't stop harassing and trying to manipulate you after the divorce. They may ask you how your day has been, and if you answer back, giving them details about how your day has been, they will store that information to be later used against you.

Keep the details of your personal life away from them, and don't fall into the trap of explaining things to them. Don't tell them what you are up to or how you are feeling about the divorce. Only talk about vital issues relating to your children.

Keep to your set boundaries and don't make any exceptions. If you don't, they will be all over you trying to manipulate you and get more information to use against you. Stay consistent with your decisions. Ensure that they know what your boundaries are and that you won't change them.

Even if they try to turn your children against you after the divorce, don't worry about that. They will tell lies and accuse you of things you didn't do just to get your children's attention, but hold on and support your children no matter what happens. The truth will come out sooner or later.

Getting through the divorce will be a battle, but everything will soon be over. Just make your plans and stick to them no matter the cost. You must keep in mind that you can't reason with a narcissist, so don't even try to do that.

CHAPTER SEVEN

Life after Divorce from a Narcissist

Life won't be easy after divorcing your narcissistic partner, but it can certainly get better.

There was a time when Aristotle believed that the earth was the center of the solar system and that we earthlings had the planetary bodies revolving around us. As someone who has been married to a narcissist, you already know that they have a similar belief about their position in the universe. They believe that everything and everyone else in the world revolves around them.

They see themselves as the brightest star, so they desire to be praised. Your best will never be enough for them, and their inflated sense of self can never be satisfied. They are just painfully exhausting.

Is it possible for you to truly move on with your life after divorcing your narcissistic spouse? Can you get over the abuse they inflicted on you and have your life return to the way it was before you married them?

You couldn't last "till death do us part" with your narcissistic spouse, and you should know that life after the divorce is not going to be easy too.

A marriage relationship needs equality, collaboration, and empathy to work, so it is understandable why being married to a narcissist can cause problems in marriage.

If you are trying to cope with life after divorce from your narcissistic partner, you already know what being married to them feels like.

But, if you are in the divorce process, you may already be getting to know more about your ex's manipulation skills and wondering if they will even prevent the divorce.

Let us summarize the tell-tale traits of a narcissist, before discussing the realities of life after divorcing a narcissist.

They Won't Walk a Mile in Your Shoes

They expect attention to be given to them, and they also want to be praised all the time. They feel they are entitled to it, and if they don't get it, they get aggressive. The only feelings that matter to them are their own. No one else's feelings matter and they will never even walk a mile in your shoes.

They Lack Accountability

Narcissists are quick to dish out blame for what goes wrong, but they take all the credit for what goes right. Every disagreement or failure is never their own fault. It is always someone else's fault.

They Demand Perfection

They expect everyone else to stick to their own terms because they believe they are perfect.

They Are Bullies

We all know that narcissists bully because they have inferiority complex. Their habit of belittling and intimidating others is a defense mechanism to keep them from realizing the truth of who they really are.

They neither Listen nor Care

For narcissists, the only opinion that matters is theirs. They won't be bothered by the needs of others. It is always all about them.

They Are Incapable Of Emotional Intimacy

Narcissists can paint an exciting picture of how great your life will be with them. They will lure you with a dreamy picture of all the possibilities of life with them. They can do all these with their charming nature, but when you say something contrary to their own opinion or stop the flow of flattery, you become an enemy to them. Don't expect them to have any relationship-building qualities like empathy, vulnerability, compassion, or compromise.

Life after divorcing your partner may not be entirely different from the way it was when you were living with them because you have already experienced their behavior firsthand. You already know that they never see the error in the things they do, and they never care about the consequences too.

After divorce, what happens, where it happens, and when it happens may change, but how it happens still remains the same.

You can learn how to reclaim your life and move on after divorcing a narcissist.

There are brutal realities that may define your life after divorce from a narcissist. Let us discuss them.

You May Still Be Confused

They are masters at using mood swings, double standards, and criticism to get what they want. They are very good at hiding behind a charming public image to make you look like you are the bad guy to others.

You May Still Have Self-doubt

You may still doubt yourself and not trust yourself to live your life on your own yet. You will continue questioning your judgment. Narcissists chip away at your convictions, confidence, and self-esteem gradually with denials, insults, and lies.

Your Narcissistic Ex Will Not Change

Your narcissist ex won't change towards you overnight just because you are no longer married to them. Don't expect life after the divorce to be total freedom for you. Narcissists never stop seeking power and control, so don't be surprised if your ex comes after you with threats, lies and sending abusive messages.

Your Ex Won't Just Disappear From Your Life Forever

If you have children together, there is no way you won't be seeing your ex after the divorce. It will be left for you to set clear boundaries and have your reliable support group.

A narcissist is an energy vampire, and your divorce has denied them access to their immediate blood supply. They're not afraid of filing false charges or ignoring court orders. They will create chaos for you and even your kids, just to keep themselves in your life.

It May Take Some time Before You Can Stand Up For Yourself

You will start experiencing the freedom of self-expression after the divorce because your ex won't always be around you to mock you, yell at you, or shut you down. Whenever you said "no" or shared your opinion, you were faced with negative consequences while you were still married to your ex. But things are different now. There is nothing like being ignored or yelled at, and you can confidently share your feelings with anyone. You may be hesitating to share your feelings or voice out your opinions, but as you get used to life after the divorce, you will realize that you now have the opportunity to stand up to anyone and be free again.

When you start enjoying the freedom of expression again, you will embrace the changes in your life without fear.

Unless Others Live It, They May Not Understand It

It can be difficult for people to really understand the extent of the emotional and psychological abuse someone is suffering. Anyone who has experienced it won't ask you, "Why didn't you just leave?" they already understand the experience of the psychological war zone; they may not be able to explain it in clear words, but they understand the feeling.

Those people you really want to understand what you are going through may not understand. They may only see the negative consequences it has on you, but they may not know how to talk to you about it.

This is where the help of a professional who can offer you support is needed. They will help you cope with the divorce and give you the encouragement you need to carry on with your life.

Divorcing a narcissist can be as energy-draining as the marriage itself. Divorce doesn't automatically catapult you into freedom and a healthy relationship, but you at least have the opportunity to turn a new page and move on with your life.

Now that you are separating from your spouse, who is a defensive, falsely, perfect narcissist, you can have the freedom to make new choices that will lead to new relationships.

Finally, you can embrace the person you used to be before meeting your ex; you can become the person with empathy and enjoy the safety you have missed until now.

CHAPTER EIGHT

Emotional Survival

Since your narcissistic spouse is self-serving and selfish, how do you get through a divorce unscathed? How do you survive it emotionally?

Your spouse exhibits symptoms of narcissism which includes a lack of conscience, manipulation, extreme self-centeredness, and jealously of others' success.

When a divorcing couple is made up of one reasonable spouse and one narcissistic spouse, enormous conflict can be created singlehandedly by the narcissistic spouse. The reasonable spouse can go into defense mode to protect them and their children from the negative actions of the narcissist.

Others may be seeing the reasonable spouse as the initiator of the conflict, but in the real sense of it, they are only trying to stay protected from their narcissist spouse who is tapping into the divorce opportunity to bully them and their children using the legal system.

The behavior of the narcissist may be hidden from others during the marriage, but when the divorce process starts, it can be quite evident that they have the personality disorder and they won't play fair when they feel like they are being backed into a corner.

Not many people are well equipped when divorcing a narcissist. They go into the divorce process expecting what they experienced during the marriage only to be faced by an enemy who will stop at nothing to win what they see as a war.

Staying emotionally level-headed will definitely be difficult for you when the divorce process turns into a war between you both. The only way you can survive the war is to be mentally and emotionally prepared for anything your narcissistic spouse may throw your way. When you realize who you are dealing with and get yourself prepared to go to battle, you will roll up your sleeves and go to war when the need arises.

Characteristics of a Narcissist

- The narcissist is successful and charismatic
- The narcissist lacks the ability to feel remorse
- The narcissist is known to have no conscience
- The narcissist always has a tremendous need to control you and the situation
- The narcissist can pretend to hold the same beliefs as you just because they want to impress you. Their values are situational. If you believe something is wrong, so do they and this is done just to make them appear to have similar beliefs as you
- The narcissist manipulates and pretends to care
- The narcissist is emotionally unavailable

- The narcissist hangs onto resentment
- The narcissist always feels misunderstood
- The narcissist doesn't care about solving marital problems. Things must be done their own way.

When divorcing a narcissist, they don't care about all the years they have spent with you in marriage. Normal people remember the past and it makes them do things with fairness during the divorce. They remember the valuable memories shared together, but the narcissist doesn't; everything is all gone to them.

The narcissist can do terrible things to you while looking sincere and generating goodwill among the community.

How to Stay Safe and Survive the Divorce Emotionally

Your narcissistic spouse will refuse to accept that their control over your life is over, and they will do anything to remain in control. Having children with them is an avenue they can use to remain in control. They will attempt to control how child visitation is done; they will try to control other aspects of co-parenting and even child support.

Your response to your ex determines how much they abuse you emotionally, financially, and maybe even domestically. If you get sympathetic towards them after the divorce, they will tap into your emotions and strike you hard with more of their abusive behavior.

You can protect yourself by having an attorney who is willing to do all it takes to stand by your side during the divorce, and by also showing no assign of weakness when your spouse attempts to throw you off balance.

Here are some tactics that will help you stay safe and survive the divorce emotionally.

Study Your Role in the Conflict

Every time you respond to your ex, you give them the opportunity to attempt to control and manipulate you. Realize that they want you to be confused at this stage.

Ensure that you take care of your emotional health so that you don't find yourself confused about whether you are the problem or your spouse. Realize that they want you to be confused at this stage.

You can't change people's behaviors; you can only change the way you respond to them. Narcissists are always getting on your nerves to get you to react negatively to them, so ensure that you monitor your response to them. You must realize that whatever they do to you is not really about you; it is about them. They are making you feel fear, guilt, or shame in an attempt to make themselves feel better. Narcissists project their own fears, guilt, and shame onto you, but you put it back onto them when you refuse to challenge them or retaliate.

Deal With the Reality of the Situation

Narcissists live in their own made up world where everything is unreal with them desiring to be someone they are not. Their world is a fantasy one, so it is wise that you see them for who they really are and not whom you wish they were.

The more you do your best to find the good in a narcissist and to bring it out, the more they will take advantage of you. Once they try to dismiss and belittle you, but you ignore them and appreciate your own self-worth, you won't fall into their trap of trying to make you doubt your own value.

Stand Your Ground

Narcissists don't respect boundaries and the needs of others. They believe that your needs are not as important as theirs. It is unacceptable for people to disagree with them because they feel that they are more intelligent than everyone else therefore they don't respect the boundaries and needs of others.

Since you can't force a narcissist to respect your boundaries, you can however make a firm decision refusing to allow them to cross your boundaries. If they don't respect your boundaries, they will cause you unnecessary stress during the divorce process, so you need to make them understand what you will allow and what you won't.

Trying to control your ex's behavior doesn't mean that you have successfully set boundaries. Confronting them also doesn't work because you will find yourself playing into their game the more you confront them.

You should be communicating in a manner that is free of disrespect, manipulation, and conflict. When setting boundaries, you must refuse to communicate with them if they are being disrespectful, manipulative or if it is causing conflict. You can even refuse physical communication and insist that all communication must be done via email and let them know that they won't get any response from you if the communication belittles you or dismisses your needs.

While trying to separate yourself from the narcissist, they will definitely push back against the boundaries that you have set and try to pull you back into the toxic relationship, but you must stand your ground and refuse to give in to their demands if you really want to put an end to the disrespect and cycle of abuse.

Keep the Right People around You

You can go to family and friends for advice and support during your divorce. They may not fully understand the uniqueness of your situation when you tell them what you are dealing with.

This is why it is important that you hire a divorce attorney who is experienced with dealing with issues related to narcissistic personality disorder to guide you through your divorce process. Getting a therapist that will help you work through your feelings is also good. A therapist that understands these issues better can help you set boundaries and stick with them. They will help you understand your role in the conflict and point out what is real and what isn't real.

Keeping the right people around you is important because the people you go to for help will play a huge role in how you navigate divorce from your narcissistic partner.

One of the narcissist's strategies is to hide behind the mask of concern for you and your children and do their fake acts. Remember that they only care about themselves, so whatever act of concern they may be putting on is just to manipulate you.

The divorce will even be more traumatic than the marriage itself. Narcissists will not just go quiet once the marriage is over; they will find a way to use the legal system to their favor. It will be yet another weapon in their arsenal of manipulation.

They will see the divorce as another means of abusing you and no lie is too big for them to tell.

Disregard The Narcissist's Version of History

Divorces that were amicable even bring out the worst in people. Some spouses often find themselves wondering if they ever really knew the person they married and lived with for many years at all.

It is difficult for them to face the truth, and believe that their spouse has been lying to them all along.

Narcissists however show you their behavior in the marriage, but you will still need to go back and revisit what you thought you knew about your partner to better prepare yourself for court.

Disregard their own version of history as they cannot be trusted, and get yourself acquainted with everything from the beginning of the relationship, as you never know what information may be useful to you in court.

Don't Trust Their Acts of Compassion

Know that your narcissistic spouse is not under any obligation to treat you right after the divorce.

They need a constant supply of love and validation from you, but as soon as the marriage is over, you are no longer of any use to them, so don't expect any form of respect from them.

As a result, whatever they do that looks like they are showing concern or compassion for your well-being shouldn't be trusted completely; such acts should be viewed with suspicion as there is definitely a hidden motive behind it.

They may pretend to be concerned about you and your children, but you must be prepared to tackle all of that.

Strip Your Narcissist of Their Power

The best way to strip your narcissist of their power is by ignoring them and refusing to engage at all. You weaken them when you don't engage with them because they will be expecting you to argue with them to create drama that they love.

Don't Fall For Your Narcissist's Carefully Planned Script

Narcissists are good at diverting conversation from the topic at hand to some other topic. They don't discuss the problems raised; instead they divert the conversation to something else they think you have done, and which is completely unrelated to the topic at hand.

Narcissists have a pattern of diversion. They have a script they are following, and it is difficult to unravel their script.

Keep your attention focused on real issues instead of constantly responding to their accusations. Don't be caught off guard by their diversionary techniques; dismiss their accusations so you can use your energy for important things.

Don't Expect Your Narcissist to Co-Parent

Co-parenting will be used by your narcissist as a weapon to keep coming around you to manipulate you.

The legal system may glorify co-parenting, but it is wise for you to keep your life separate from your ex and communicate only when it is absolutely necessary to.

Take control over your life and don't give them back the power. Don't agree to joint birthday celebrations, holidays, or even going out together for events. Keep your distance from them.

Be a great parent to your children and ensure that they feel supported, loved, and validated when they are with you.

Don't Give In When You Are Too Tired To Go On

Narcissists are just like wolves. They get successful by getting you exhausted, and wearing you down to the point where you get too tired with no energy left to run. They are hoping to see you lose your strength once they succeed in draining your energy so that you can stop running and give up the fight.

You must realize that your narcissist is just trying to wear you down on purpose. If you give up the fight now, you will regret it years later once you have recovered and regained your lost strength.

Stop Letting Your Emotions Make Decisions For You

It is easy to look at divorce from an emotional perspective when you are heartbroken or disillusioned.

However, it is wise for you to remove emotion from the process, so you can do the right thing for your well-being, because true narcissists take divorce as war. Know that you are your partner's enemy and they want you defeated.

Even though you may be unable to make those important decisions for your future and truly begin the healing process, you have to do your best to move on with your life. Don't stay overwhelmed by your pain; a narcissist lacks empathy and they will exploit your weakness and even battle you if they have to.

Put your emotions aside when it is time to legally separate. You can cry all the tears you want, but leave your heart out of it and use only your mind when figuring out those details that will determine how you'll live the rest of your life after the divorce papers are signed.

Do not engage your narcissistic spouse with an emotional response because emotions can easily run high during divorce cases, and divorcing a narcissist takes it to another level.

A divorce must become a business transaction when it comes to assets. Challenges are also encountered when it comes to child custody and parenting time.

Divorcing a narcissistic spouse comes with many challenges, but one effective way to overcome the challenges is to face your fears. Whatever evidence you gather, you and your attorney should make sure that it is in the best interests of the children, so the strategy and path you choose should lead you to obtaining child custody and parenting time orders that are consistent with it.

Refuse to get yourself sucked into your spouse's attempts to intimidate you, abuse you emotionally, and instill fear in you; this way you will disarm them.

It may be easier said than done, but you don't want to allow your emotions and not your mind to make decisions for you during the divorce proceeding. You will be sending your divorce down a dangerous path, so don't be your own worst enemy. Do what is best for you and your children.

If you refuse to cooperate with your lawyer and you let your emotions control you, you may not be happy with the consequences. Don't make mistakes that will cause your divorce to go off the rails.

Ensure that your negotiations are limited to what is necessary and reasonable. Your narcissistic spouse will be disarmed in court when they lose control of the decision-making and it is left to an experienced family law judge who is not intimidated by your narcissist's nonsense.

I'm sure any sane person would prefer a reasonable resolution in a divorce compared to litigation, but for a reasonable resolution to happen, both spouses need to have a meeting of minds, which means a reasonable compromise.

However, compromise is hard to reach when divorcing a narcissist and it is simply impossible to achieve that. What makes it so difficult is because narcissists only have one perspective, which is their own. Negotiations become difficult when one partner only sees their perspective and believes every other perspective is wrong.

When reasonable attempts have been made to settle issues and it becomes clear that you are wasting your time, then you should stop. If you continue, the case can drag on for a very long time.

Stop Being the Narcissist's Victim

Victims of abuse are usually taught that they should develop the courage to rise above it and become emotionally and psychologically strong. It is very easy for you to call yourself the narcissist's victim and then give up and stop trying to put an end to the emotional, psychological, or physical abuse you are going through.

You can make good choices for yourself and your children once you recognize that you have a choice; you can then take the necessary steps to become safe from abuse.

Once all this is over, you will be able to pass on what you have learned to others who are dealing with similar situations and are almost giving up.

Have No Tolerance for Violations

Your lawyer should be able to come up with options that work best for your family during the divorce. Ensure that custody exchanges don't happen in a deserted place; custody exchanges should happen in a public place and communication should be limited to only what is necessary. Don't give room for any manipulation and make sure that you record conversations so that you can have evidence in case of any threats from your spouse.

If your spouse refused to comply with a court order, you can bring it to the attention of the court. You can handle this by filing a contempt motion and requesting attorney's fees. Once they see that you will not tolerate this behavior, they may think twice about violating court orders in the future.

CHAPTER NINE

Safeguarding Yourself

Now that the divorce from your narcissistic partner is over, it is time for you to pay attention to yourself. Repair and self-care should be on your mind. You may have difficulty setting boundaries because of the fear of repercussions.

The emotional, physical and financial abuse you suffered in the hands of the narcissist made you question your reality and get used to tolerating mistreatment.

If you have to co-parent, then you have to do all it takes to psychologically separate yourself from your ex so that you can recover your sense of self. You can still struggle with the effects of the narcissistic abuse even though you never had children with your ex to make you have reasons to see them again.

Let us discuss the ways in which you can heal and protect yourself after divorcing a narcissist.

Know What to Expect

Narcissists don't care about putting the children first in whatever they do after a divorce. They also don't care about getting over the divorce. They are always so quick to project their shortcomings on you because they are incapable of taking accountability for their own actions. They can't accept that they might have imperfections, so everything that goes wrong in the relationship is automatically your fault. They will blame you for everything. The marriage that ended is your fault; the issue with co-parenting is also your fault. They don't do well with criticisms. Their blaming habit makes them feel superior, so know what to expect.

Trust Yourself

Don't go wasting your time and energy, trying to talk sense to a narcissist. You already know the truth about your ex, and those closest to you also know the truth. Even if a team of mental health experts get together and explain to your ex what is wrong with them, they still wouldn't change their behavior, so don't' allow their behavior to make you question your reality. You will only end up getting exhausted, so the best you can do is to direct your energy towards rebuilding your own life.

Set Boundaries

Now that you have divorced your partner, you have to start setting limits and adhering to them. The reason your self-esteem was seriously crushed during your marriage was because your partner disregarded your rights, and your boundaries were not respected. You made it easier for your ex to abuse you because you couldn't stick to your guns.

When co-parenting is causing conflict, it is best to use the principles of parallel parenting to help enforce boundaries. Parallel parenting involves divorced parents co-parenting by disengaging from each other to enable them to have limited contact with each other in situations where they are unable to communicate respectfully.

Practice Effective Communication

Avoid exchanging lengthy texts and emails with your ex; doing this gives them access to attack you verbally. You don't need to communicate with them all the time; only communicate when it is necessary and be brief and informative when you do. Don't get caught up in any argument or protracted negotiation. Your narcissist wants to get you hooked by gradually luring you into conversations with them, and then breaking you emotionally, so be guarded.

Focus On Healing

You spent years of your life doing what your narcissist wanted; this is the time to do what you really want to do. Even though you need to communicate with each other because you are co-parenting, know that you don't have any marital relationship anymore. Concentrate on healing and not dwelling on the past.

What you should be doing now is nurturing your relationships with friends and family, practicing self-care, and going to therapy. You can create a meaningful future for yourself if you can get clear on your values and goals.

Stop Feeling, Start Thinking

Divorce is the ultimate opportunity for your narcissist to showcase themselves as a victim and a martyr. You need to get yourself prepared for all the drama that the divorce will bring.

They will finally get the opportunity to prove to the world that you are a horrible person and parent. The worst you can do at this point is to react emotionally to their drama because your emotions are irrelevant. Once you start reacting emotionally to them, you start losing your ground. So stop feeling and start thinking.

Once you don't have a strategy, and you do whatever comes to your mind during the divorce, you will end up getting all your energy drained and surrendering. You will find yourself saying, "I can't take this anymore, I give up" because, without a properly thought out plan in place, you have already set yourself up for failure and mental breakdown.

A person who has been emotionally abused for years doesn't sound like a person who can fight to

the end, so to avoid that, let us discuss some guidelines that will help you.

Take Your Time

You don't need to hire an attorney the same day you decide to start the divorce process. Take your time to go all out and interview a few professionals to find the person that is best suited to help you with your case. Don't be in a rush as the hiring process is a very important step, so there should be an interview process, and it should be carefully done. After interviewing a few professionals, you can then hire the best for your situation.

Listen and Ask Questions

Ensure that you have reasonable expectations. You shouldn't have preconceived notions of how the whole process should go. Get yourself educated on how the divorce process should go so that you don't find yourself trying to wrongfully control the process with the ideas that you have already thought out. Listen when issues are being discussed and ask questions to understand what is being said before talking about it.

Make a list of important questions about the divorce that you need answers to and take it to your attorney. You can ask questions about what will happen to the house after your divorce, what mistakes your attorney has seen people make, and what laws exist.

Your attorney will explain the entire process to you and provide you with clear answers to your most pressing questions, so make a list of your questions and concerns.

Identify What the End Goal Is

Make your attorney know what your end goal is so that they can help you with it. Don't go fighting over unnecessary issues when you should be using your time wisely.

Your narcissist will definitely want you to pay attention to everything they are throwing your way so you can react. So, before you go wasting $50 on a $100 issue, think again.

Focus on Your Narcissist's Actions

Focus on what your spouse is doing and not on who they are. If you think you already know them and what they will do next, be prepared to get shocked. Make up your mind to act according to their present actions.

Battle Reasonably

Don't become unreasonable to the point where you turn yourself into a narcissist because you are battling one. Work with the facts you have at hand and handle the settlements or let the court make the decisions. You battle them by thinking reasonably. You don't become a narcissist to battle a narcissist.

Financial Strategies for Divorcing a Narcissist

We know that true narcissists believe that rules do not apply to them because they think they are above the law; this makes life difficult for anyone dealing with them. You can't get them to do simple things because they will make a big issue out of a small one. They are just difficult to deal with.

You need to get yourself prepared for the financial aspects of divorcing your narcissistic spouse. Be prepared for a long, drawn-out fight, as the narcissist thrives on the adversarial nature of litigation. The first thing you need to do to prepare for this is to make plans on how you will fund this litigation.

During the divorce, they will refuse to negotiate as they want things done on their own terms. They will also refuse to provide financial information and documents.

Don't get surprised when you see them refusing to listen to their own lawyer and defying court orders. Keep it in mind that they can also use your children as pawns if it can help them manipulate the legal system.

Other abusive men have feelings of regret for their abusive behavior. However, narcissists feel no remorse because they feel that they are the one who should be apologized to for wrongful behavior. They can be exceedingly emotionally and verbally abusive even though they may not physically abuse you.

If you are divorcing a narcissistic spouse, here are critical financial preparations you should make.

Have Enough Funds on Hand and Start Building Credit

You will have to be prepared to face a long, drawn-out battle with your spouse because you can be sure that they will have tactics already planned out. Having enough cash ready for the war is necessary.

In case you will need to take a personal loan or need access to credit, ensure that your credit is in top shape. Building credit is important for you, so if you didn't have a strong credit history before, you should get a starter credit card for your everyday purchases to help you start building credit. Always do your best to pay your bills on time, as it is an important factor in establishing credit.

Get a credit card that is in your own name if you don't already have one, start making small purchases every month, then ensure that you pay the balance off in full to help you build your credit history.

Get Your Financial Paperwork in Order

You must get your financial paperwork in order before the divorce process starts because your narcissistic spouse will attempt to hide assets from you and likely refuse to give you any required documents when you ask them. So before the divorce gets underway, collect all account numbers and get copies of all financial documents.

Ensure that documents include retirement accounts, credit card accounts, deeds, stocks, and tax returns should be included.

Give yourself enough time to put together all the financial and legal documents you will need for the divorce and remember to make copies of them. After getting the paperwork in order, store all the documents in a safe place and away from your narcissistic spouse's reach.

Get a Divorce Financial Planner

You already know that it is essential for you to get a skilled attorney who has experience with domestic abuse and division of marital property to handle your divorce.

You need a financial expert on your team, so hiring a divorce financial planner who has the training and experience to guide and help you ensure your financial security is also recommended.

Your narcissistic partner will be vindictive and hurtful, and they'll thrive on it, so ensure that you get your emotional support system in place.

You are ready to move on with the divorce process once you have assembled your team, your paperwork is in intact, and you have your money also ready.

Once the divorce has been initiated, remember to keep direct communication with your spouse to a fact-based, dispassionate minimum.

Divorcing your narcissist may be the most difficult thing you will ever do, but you will succeed if you take time out to plan for it.

Things Not To Do When Divorcing a Narcissist

When trying to get out of a relationship with a narcissist, negotiating how to divide your assets with your spouse may be the very last thing on your mind. Your physical safety may seem more important than thinking about assets because you need to look out for your well-being for the sake of your children. Whatever you take away from the marriage will help you establish a financially stable home for your children, so don't bother about what your spouse says or does.

Your spouse can say and do all sorts of crazy and embarrassing things that you will fall for. They can use their status to bully and threaten you, but when you wrap your head around the fact that the narcissist believes that they are the victim and everything wrong is your fault, you will be able to take your emotions out of it and make the right decisions.

Your spouse may tell you that you'll get nothing if you pushed for part of the marriage assets. They may also tell you that they will take your children away from you or that you are not entitled to child support.

You may have forgotten how much it actually cost to set up your household, but it is crucial that you take a comprehensive look at your financial situation and make the necessary plans.

When dividing your assets with your narcissistic spouse, don't do the following things:

Don't Get Emotional

Don't allow yourself to get manipulated into getting emotional. Stick to the business at hand, which is the dividing of the assets.

Don't Assume That Your Spouse Will Consider the Kids and Act Justly

Your narcissistic spouse will only look out for themselves and won't act in the best interest of the children, so don't assume that they will act justly and be nice.

Don't Just Walk Away

You may start thinking that everything your spouse has been telling you about yourself is true. You may also think that if you let them win, the abuse will stop, but their win will only make them happy for a short period of time, so don't just walk away; complete the divorce process and move on with your life.

Don't Be Too Nice To Take All of the Debt

A debt that is unsecured is a shared liability, not just the person whose name the debt is in, so don't just take all of the debt.

Don't Settle For Less than Half of Your Assets

You may have been the breadwinner of the family, bought your first home, and your income kept the family afloat during your spouse's lean years. Also, you may have greatly supported your spouse during the early years of your marriage, but had to quit your job after some years into the marriage so that you can have enough time to raise the kids. So, don't settle for less than half of your assets, even though your spouse feels you are not entitled to anything.

Don't Underestimate the Value of Any Property

Know that rental properties are worth more than just their actual value, so ensure that you do not underestimate the value of any property.

Don't Forget To Evaluate Pension Plans and Other Retirement Funds

Remember to evaluate pension plans and other retirement funds as it is necessary to do that.

Don't Leave Out Long-term Financial Needs

Don't give up child support. Your long-term financial health and also the needs of your kids should not be forgotten. Your children will need to go to college. The cost of taking care of the kids should not be underestimated. School supplies, clothes, extracurricular activities, and school projects all require money, so don't leave anything off the list. Ensure that you also plan for cars and insurance for those cars.

Don't Confuse Community Property and Separate Property

You should know the difference between community property and separate property, so don't confuse the two.

Don't Take Your Partner's Word for It

Ensure that you get a business valuation and have someone seriously look at all the assets and financial documents if your partner owns a business.

Don't Let Your Partner Wear You Down

Even if it isn't contentious, the whole thing is exhausting. It's tempting for you to just throw your hands in the air and be done. Find something else like exercise to do instead, or call your friends. Keep yourself busy with self-care and then take another look at the financials.

Don't Shoot For Timelines That Are Unreasonable

Putting everything together takes time, so don't shoot for unreasonable timelines. You are going to be in for a long battle since you are dealing with a narcissist, and know that it will be draining too.

Don't Forget About Taxes and Deductions

During filing, issues like which spouse claims which child on their taxes needs to be clearly laid out in the divorce.

Your narcissistic partner may try to make you feel guilty, but remember that you have to continue taking care of your children, so don't walk away from anything. You can't divide something you don't know about, so it is reasonable to take a comprehensive look at your financial affairs.

Know that your lawyer is not your financial advisor. They can only advise you based on their experiences, but your financial advisor has the experience to handle any complicated financial situation you may have.

Keeping your emotions in check is crucial when divorcing a narcissist. You must realize that this is not about revenge; it is about dividing the assets from the marriage equitably so that the children can have two financially secure homes as they grow up.

CHAPTER TEN

Moving on After Divorce from a Narcissist

It is quite dreadful being in a marriage relationship with a narcissist, but ending the relationship and starting a new life on your own is often a daunting task. Don't be guided by your emotions but rather think logically and map out the strategy to follow after divorcing your narcissist.

When a narcissistic spouse threatens their partner and the safety of the children, in such cases, many others in such a situation would leave the relationship. Getting out of this toxic relationship can take time.

Narcissists feel entitled to certain privileges, so if their partner or children don't give them the kind of attention, admiration, or respect they desire, they may subject them to emotional punishment.

So, one important part of healing after divorcing a narcissist is setting boundaries and protecting yourself and your children from them. Don't expect them to keep your children's best interests in mind or to negotiate fairly because they lack empathy and don't care about others.

In most cases, co-parenting with a narcissist is problematic because their attention is focused mostly on themselves and not really on the needs of the children, so this is not a realistic expectation. You will probably be engaged in a battle while attempting to co-parent with a narcissist. Being authentic with your ex isn't a wise thing to do. Limited contact and well-set boundaries are necessary to effectively manage a high-conflict divorce.

We know that narcissists are unremorseful and have a complete disregard and contempt for others. They may even offer excuses for certain behaviors they have portrayed, but don't allow yourself to get carried away and deceived by their apologies because they'll never be genuinely remorseful. Their inflated sense of entitlement and self-esteem is unrelated to real talent or accomplishments, so they can easily feel jealous or threatened when you or their children give others attention.

It is still best that you assess the degree of your partner's narcissism. In certain circumstances, where a narcissist is a threat to you and your children's safety and stability, the relationship with them isn't worth fighting for.

When dealing with a narcissist, you must ensure that you make safety your first and foremost priority, especially if they are beginning to threaten you more and becoming more violent or explosive. Ensure that you are not alone with them. Before you plan your exit strategy, put the safety of yourself and your children first if you see that your partner is perpetually verbally or emotionally abusive.

Instead of blaming yourself for marrying a narcissist in the first place, redirect your focus from the narcissist to yourself and your healing. You have become used to being focused on them and looking out for the next thing they are going to do. It's time to focus on only what is within your power to control, which is your own behavior.

After ending the toxic relationship, you can regain control of your life. It will be difficult, but you can achieve it if you are willing to work at it using the strategies below.

Focus On Your Behavior, Which Is the Only Thing You Can Control

Your happiness is in your hands, and you alone are responsible for it. If you are not comfortable with doing something, don't allow your ex to persuade you into doing it. Don't do it just because you want to maintain peace. Adopt a formal style of communication with them if you have to.

Minimize Contact with Your Ex

Get yourself prepared to write a script that you can use when talking with your ex. Ensure that you only use a few words and stick with it because high-conflict personalities thrive on the possibility of combat.

For instance, if they are trying to persuade you and talking about reuniting with you again, just respond and say, "I tried to make our marriage work. Everything is still the same and nothing has changed, so it's not healthy for us to reunite. I wish you the best with your life."

Don't apologize for wrongdoing in the marriage or express genuine emotion to your ex. If your ex is an abusive narcissist and you express genuine emotion to them or apologize for wrongdoing in the marriage, they might use it against you if they interpret it as a sign of your incompetence. Refuse to tolerate denigrating or abusive behavior from your narcissistic ex.

You can decide to have a family member or a close friend around when you talk to your ex. Ensure to save all abusive text messages or emails received from your ex.

Ensure That You Have Plenty of Support

Ensure that you ask a therapist if they have experience with cognitive behavior therapy (CBT). Therapists who have the experience are usually the most successful when it comes to dealing with persons who are survivors of a relationship with a narcissist.

People with codependent traits can easily get attracted to narcissists, and this is not uncommon. Your happiness should be of utmost concern to you; that is why it is essential that you let go of the feelings weighing you down.

Codependents are consumed with the desires of others, and they are giving people. However, they find it difficult to emotionally disconnect from romantic relationships with narcissists even though they are self-centered, controlling, and harmful to them.

During your counseling sessions, you can discuss ways that you can set boundaries with your narcissistic ex; this will also prevent you from giving up your power and getting involved in a self-defeating pattern of relating with a new partner.

You deserve a happiness filled life, so it is crucial that you take a critical and honest look at the impacts of your ex's behavior on you and your children. Once you have made up your mind and accepted that you can only control your own behavior without allowing a narcissistic ex to influence your decisions, you will see a great improvement in your life.

The Armor of Healing

If you have been with a narcissist for a long time, you will likely have a period when you wonder if you will ever be free to be yourself again. Massive success is the best revenge for any belittlement you must have suffered in the hands of your ex-partner. When the relationship has really harmed you, the wise thing to do is to take healing inside. Reclaiming your sense of self and life is best for you at this time.

The deepness of your hurt depends on a lot of factors or things that are unique to you. These factors include your family background, your strength when you first started the relationship with your narcissistic partner, the length of the relationship, and how bad the relationship was. You may have likely had a lack of belief and trust in yourself, and also had your self-esteem damaged.

Most partners of narcissists have been diagnosed with post-traumatic stress disorder caused by extreme verbal, emotional, and psychological abuse. Some of them have also suffered physical and sexual abuse.

Some close friends and family members will not understand the extent of the pain or damage you have suffered in the marriage, because the narcissists appear well to the outside world. It is best that you do not look to the people who do not understand the extent of your pain for sympathy or advice. Listen to your gut and honor your feelings.

Ensure that you have a recovery program that will enable you and your children to move forward successfully.

Some friends and family members will say things like "just get over it and move on"; they are quite right, and you are not going to remain a victim forever, but you can't just move on without first recovering from the damage you suffered. Your number one goal is to move on, but you must attend to your emotional baggage first. Leaving your feelings unattended to will weigh you down and slow down the development of your new life.

When you get out of a horrible marriage with a person who has dragged your self-esteem in the mud for years, expect to have court battles, finance wars, and custody issues with them. It takes a bite out of you and makes you feel like you have to be refurbished like a car that is wrecked.

Despite all that you may be feeling, your friends and family members can keep saying that you should stop dwelling on the past and get over it. As easy as they may think it is, it really isn't that easy to just get over it. Those feelings and trauma will continuously haunt you years after you have divorced your partner and even started a new relationship if you don't first address the issues.

A road map to healing will be of help to you. You first need to accept what has happened and then take time off to grieve. You can then psychologically separate yourself from your ex. The next thing to do is to work at becoming your authentic self. After this, you can move over to dealing with your ex while recovering from the pain of the breakup. Finally, the legacy of distorted love can come to an end.

Picking up the Pieces

You may be in a marriage with a narcissist for some months before you first catch them in a huge lie that will threaten your livelihood. During all your years of being married to a compulsive liar, you will lose yourself. This can change you, and you can gradually become someone that you are not. You may become judgmental, snappy, angry, or rude.

Being married to someone with these narcissistic traits is a form of emotional and psychological abuse that we don't often discuss because your self-esteem gets shattered by lies, deceit, manipulation, and control. The experience is often crippling and humiliating. You even spend many nights crying yourself to sleep and wondering what could be done to make yourself feel whole again. You weep for the loss of yourself.

After spending years of abuse in the hands of a compulsive liar, you will need to find some mechanisms to cope and get back the former self you have lost to the abuse.

We know that a narcissist changes their identity frequently and uses others for their own benefit.

Living with them tears at the very fiber of your being and forces you into a shadow of the person you know you can be. You are often made out to be "the crazy one", making you question yourself and your own sanity.

Moving on and finding yourself again will require you picking up the pieces of your life with these tips:

Accept

Accept who you are and the situation. You may want to analyze everything, self-criticize, and blame yourself, but you aren't the cause of everything that went wrong. You just need to recognize that you were married to a person with a personality disorder, and it isn't your fault that they have the disorder. There is nothing you can do to change the situation.

Take Responsibility

Take some time to think about things and come to terms with the fact that you are the one who chose this person. Also, let it sink in that narcissists, and compulsive liars are often irresistible. They usually create a charming personality for themselves, and you fell for their charms.

Cut Off All Contact with Your Ex

Your ex will try to lure you back into their web of lies, and they can even move into attack mode and blame you for everything that was their fault. Remember that they do well at projecting blame onto others, so cut off all contact with them if you don't have to co-parent together.

Learn To Direct Your Kindness Inwards

We are often kind people who direct our kindness towards others. It will also benefit us if we start directing our kindness inwards.

Just Stop

When you notice that you are beating yourself up over a decision you made, just stop. Realize that you were manipulated by your ex, and you are not to blame. You can start by changing your words, and then it will change how you feel about yourself, and your self-worth will increase.

Tap Into Your Passions Again

Remember the activities that give you a sense of fulfillment and get involved with them. This is a crucial step in regaining your lost self and finding happiness again. Your newfound happiness will help you regain the confidence you have long lost.

Learn More about Spotting Liars

When you learn this, you won't be blinded to the signs of a narcissistic disorder; you will have the ability to spot them before you even enter into a new relationship with someone else.

Give Yourself Time to Breathe

You may feel unfamiliar with the transitioning from chaos to normalcy, and it can be a strange and frightening experience for you. Give yourself some time to breathe and calm down. You will need it to pick up the broken pieces of your life.

Know That It's Okay To Grieve

There is no need to be ashamed of grieving. It's definitely okay to grieve the person you used to be and whom you left behind when the relationship with your narcissistic ex began.

Take One Step Forward

Take a step towards your goal every day you wake up. It's a small step, but it's okay. When you safely make it out of your trauma, you will look back sometimes and won't believe that you were ever in a relationship with your ex. Ensure to be grateful for each day that comes.

The best you can do is to listen to your heart and follow it. Keep reminding yourself that you will be alright again.

Marrying a narcissist is something that can happen to anyone, so you are not alone in this. They search for partners who can take care of their demands and their child-like needs, and they also search for people who are compassionate, kind, and strong. They don't choose a partner who can't meet their demands.

Know that you are capable of having a healthy relationship with anyone else. Divorcing a narcissist and a compulsive liar shouldn't stop you from being open to getting to meet new people. Stay ready to meet new people, and you will learn more in the process of getting over your ex.

CHAPTER ELEVEN

Trauma Recovery

When people think about trauma, what comes to their mind is usually events like car accidents or natural disasters. But trauma doesn't only involve that; it can take many different forms.

Trauma can come to you in the form of a soul-crushing narcissistic abuse because it doesn't hit you at once. It builds gradually and ends up affecting your identity and your mental health on a very deep level that can take you years to recover from. That is why it usually takes time to recover from narcissistic abuse; it is an ongoing process, not an instantaneous event.

Healing from trauma related to narcissistic abuse requires a different approach than other traumatic events. Just like people who are working through drug or alcohol recovery, it is essential to work through the phases of trauma recovery. It is not really a fast and easy process, but at the end of it all, you will emerge a more dignified and stronger person than you were before you started experiencing narcissistic abuse.

Why Healing from Narcissistic Abuse Is Different

The complex trauma that is associated with narcissistic abuse could make you feel like you have been living in a war zone for many years. The fighting and psychological torture are terrible, and you get confined to emotional, spiritual, and even physical isolation.

As time goes on, you feel like your access to the rest of the world is being restricted, and you begin to wonder why you are going through all these while others are living in peace. You also start thinking that something must be wrong with you, and you are not alright, or this abuse wouldn't continue.

You don't get this kind of feeling with trauma related to car accidents and other events. Some people might get involved in a car accident and be broken to the point of them wondering why God would allow such an incident to happen to them. People realize that events such as car accidents and natural disasters cannot be controlled by them. They are random events that they have no power over. When earthquakes and fire outbreaks happen, people don't usually blame themselves for it. But they blame themselves when it is narcissistic abuse, and this is why the healing process is different because the abuse attacks your psyche, your sense of self, and also your spirit.

How Narcissistic Abuse Deeply Affects You

When you are trying to have a healthy and functional relationship with a personality-disordered person, it doesn't work out well; narcissistic abuse is a frequent outcome of that. A disordered person cannot really have a close relationship with anyone. It will lead to abuse.

Due to the psychological manipulation techniques such as silent treatment that your narcissist ex used on you during your marriage to them, you can develop a devastating emotional crisis.

It can start by having a heated fight every now and then with your spouse; the situation calms down, and then you just write it off and forget about it thinking it is a one-time event.

You start to see the red flags, but you ignore them. Your spouse is just in a bad mood, right? But then the fighting doesn't end; instead, its pace increases. As the fighting increases, you start to notice that you are always wrong in every scenario, even when you started talking to your spouse in a polite tone and asking for an apology or basic respect.

I'm sure you remember the many times you have tried to politely confront your narcissist spouse about something they did that hurt you only for them to unexpectedly flare up and turn the conversation into an abusive situation. You then had to apologize to them at the end of the conversation.

They treated you horribly, but they played the victim because someone else must always be the perpetrator. In the hypothetical movie that is playing inside their head, you are the antagonist while they are the protagonist.

As you go through this subtle manipulation, after weeks, months, or even years, you start to believe it without even being aware of what is happening. It impacts the way you view the people around you and yourself. You start to see yourself as someone who is worthless, can't get anything done right, and is of no use to anyone. You start seeing yourself as a person that no one can ever enjoy being around.

The Choice Point

Every choice we make creates the future we will see. There is usually a window of opportunity, called a Choice Point, every time another cycle of emotional abuse is experienced with the narcissist. In the place referred to as the Choice Point, we actually get the chance to change the negative cycles that have become recurring in our lives.

We can choose to keep making the same choices that keep us suffering in the toxic relationship, or we can choose to make a different choice. We can choose to change our mindset and our behavior.

When you are stuck in a cycle of constant fights during a narcissistic abuse, it's challenging for you to even pause and think about the situation.

We usually don't think about what we would experience in the next weeks or years if we decide not to leave the toxic relationship we are in. When you choose to stay in the relationship, you don't recognize that your decision could affect your friends, family, and even others.

Our choices will not affect only us; they go on to affect the future of our children and our grandchildren's too. Our neighborhoods, workplaces, and society are also affected by the choices we make. You will definitely experience moments of betrayal and emotional devastation during your marriage to a narcissist; this is inescapable. You will only want to stop the pain so that things can go back to the way they used to be so that you can feel better about yourself again.

We keep responding to our abusive partner's text messages in the middle of a corporate meeting without wondering if we might even be ruining our career.

Many people may overlook the narcissistic abuse thinking that they are immune from the effects until something terrible like getting fired from their job happens or even when their child commits suicide due to being fed up with being made to feel less worthy and the constant verbal assaults and fights in the family.

Our brains are headed for the worse when we experience repeated stress from emotional and verbal abuse, and we may not even recognize it.

We don't think that by staying in the toxic relationship with our narcissistic partner, we are likely setting our children up to be either codependent or narcissistic, thereby promoting generational dysfunction.

What if your narcissist has been cheating on you, and you just found out that they have been lying about almost everything and cannot be trusted with your life and that of the children? What would you do? Are you just going to sit and breathe into a paper bag to prevent yourself from hyperventilating? What can you do to fix the situation and be sane again?

Even though it is impossible to think rationally when suffering emotional abuse, you always have a choice. There may have been moments during the periods of unbearable anguish where your cognitive mind whispered to you. "I told you that this would definitely happen, but you won't listen to me".

You don't listen to your cognitive mind, but you listen to your traumatized subconscious mind. You start wondering what you can do to make your narcissist partner accountable or how you can work your way back into their good graces so that they can choose to stay with you instead of the person they are having an affair with.

These are known as your choice point events, and there are also much larger forces at play. Choice points are wake up calls, not random episodes. We need to first read the signs and then make better choices at these times.

Some choice points are very important in our lives as they are life-changing turning points. We can get our lives greatly enriched with far wiser choices if we can bring our awareness to when critical choice points are at hand.

Realize that narcissistic abuse recovery is a marathon, not a sprint.

It may sometimes take years or even decades for complex trauma from narcissistic abuse to develop. Therefore healing from a narcissistic abuse shouldn't be expected to be instantaneous, and you shouldn't believe whoever tells you that you can heal immediately too.

As years passed by, your narcissist partner slowly took away your sense of self and spirit, thereby making the healing from complex trauma an ongoing process. Complete freedom of the past may not even be an ideal goal, and people get to realize this along the way as they work through the phases of trauma recovery.

When it comes to your story, the narcissistic abuse you suffered doesn't have to make up your whole book; it can just be a chapter in your book. Working through the phases of trauma recovery is crucial.

When you experience narcissistic abuse, the effects of the complex trauma will follow you everywhere you go. It will be felt as you try to rebuild lost relationships, make new friends, seek new jobs, and even develop a new identity for yourself again. The new identity you will have will even be more compassionate, more assertive, and stronger than it was before you even met your narcissist partner. The healing process is a difficult one, but it does get better with time.

The Phases of Trauma Recovery

You may already be aware of the five stages of grief, and we know that grief is a traumatic event that gets to you on a spiritual level. Narcissistic abuse also has similar stages of healing, and it is vital that you work through each of the stages with a support system and an open heart too.

I'm sure you don't expect a person who is suffering from substance abuse to recover from it overnight, because they must work through the steps of their recovery program. Ask those recovering from drug, alcohol, or even gambling about their recovery process and they'll enlighten you about it and tell you that it's an ongoing process that continues every day, and may even continue indefinitely.

When you get to meet anyone with years of solid recovery, you'll find that they are resilient, in total control of their life and their emotions, and also living their best life.

The five stages of trauma recovery can help you through any trauma you may be experiencing after your divorce. You will be led through the stages of healing after the narcissistic abuse.

Emergency Stabilization Phase

This stage is the first phase of narcissistic abuse recovery. It is the most important phase, but also the hardest.

After going no contact from your narcissist ex, you may still be doubting and asking yourself if you actually made the right decision or not. You may still be experiencing the abuse in the form of text messages from strange numbers or even relayed messages from mutual friends.

You may have become used to the trauma because it has felt normal for a long time, so calmness and safety suddenly feel foreign to you whenever you experience it. You feel vulnerable and need reassurance and support at this time because you are still afraid that your ex will keep responding to everything you do.

During the Emergency Stabilization Phase, it is crucial that you maintain no contact with your ex or extremely modified contact if you are sharing custody. Being mature and civil is not part of your narcissist ex's personality, so if you share custody, don't have a false sense of security when they tell you that they will be honest with you or come through for the kids.

Don't allow yourself to be deceived; they will take it as an opportunity for them to continue taking advantage of you and to keep being the dictator over your life. Don't get carried away by their tricks and ulterior motives.

Because of the pull to reconnect with your partner and the addiction that develops after going through repeated traumas, the emergency stabilization phase is the most difficult to endure.

If you keep breaking No Contact, you will end up staying entangled in the toxic relationship longer than you intend to. This is the reason why maintaining No Contact with your ex should be made your top priority when you are in the healing stages after narcissistic abuse.

Punching Upwards Phase

The Punching Upwards Phase is when you start gaining your energy back after it has been drained by your narcissistic partner for so long until you can pick yourself up off the floor.

At this stage, you may find yourself experiencing surges of anger towards your ex and even yourself for staying in the relationship and allowing your ex to abuse you for so long. You might find yourself slipping back into phase one if you don't have proper support and recovery.

After going No Contact, many people feel so insecure and desperate because they have an insecure attachment style; this insecure attachment style that they have manifests as open, raw emotional wounding, as well as feelings of rejection and abandonment in the wake of narcissistic abuse.

Your attachment style may not have been largely insecure when your toxic relationship started, but it is certainly that way after the narcissistic abuse.

At the expense of their own values and interest, people who have insecure attachment styles focus on keeping their narcissist ex close to themselves. This goes to explain the reason why partners of narcissists who are victims of abuse cave into demands such as repeatedly forgiving the infidelities of the narcissist and accepting to work and handle all the bills while the narcissist frolics and plays with their other supply sources.

Because they are desperately trying to attach to their narcissist partner, this happens, and it only leads to more feelings of panic. To counteract this feeling, the only way is to find an emotional attachment figure after initiating No Contact.

This emotional attachment figure can be a family member, friend, coach, therapist, or God. This person will be the person you run to when you need to talk to someone during your period of No Contact.

The One Foot in the Door Phase

This third stage of healing after divorcing from a narcissist is very delicate. Your past still gets in the way, even when you are trying to rebuild your identity. You might even start to take some of the blame yourself and saying "they also experience abuse" or even saying, "we both treated each other badly".

Without much warning, you can revert to the earlier phases of trauma recovery at any time. It is less common than during phase two. During the entire process, support and guidance from transformational coaches and experienced professionals are really important.

You are beginning to feel confident in your decisions and in yourself, so you may even start feeling compelled to reach out to your narcissist ex on casual terms and maybe to see if they have changed or they are still the same.

In this phase, you will be dealing with the withdrawal from the biochemical addiction that formed after repeated cycles of abuse.

Your mind will try to convince you and tell you all kinds of things to make you contact your ex even though you are in withdrawal. It will tell you that things can still return to the way they used to be when you first met your spouse before the abuse started. You will begin to think about this, and for a little while, the idea will seem feasible to you as your brain brings up fragile memories of you two, leaving you with an aching desire to reach out to your ex. You will start telling yourself that you overreacted to the situation, and you should have held back. Then you will start seeking closure or an explanation.

Reaching out to your ex may seem like a good idea to you right now, but take heed because it will only set you back in your recovery, or worse, drag you right back into the cycle of abuse that you are tired of enduring. Take a look around and talk to survivors of narcissistic abuse who tried to do this and see how it ended.

Objective Analysis Phase

In this phase, you can look back at your past objectively and not even feel overwhelmed with anger or too much regret. You are now ready to help others who have suffered narcissistic abuse and are in the early phases of trauma recovery because you have spent time looking inwards and identifying emotional triggers left over from the narcissistic abuse.

You might still find yourself doubting your ability to handle issues or even having feelings of worthlessness even though you have worked so hard to rebuild your identity.

In this objective analysis phase, most survivors of narcissistic abuse suffer from the symptoms of attempted perspecticide.

Perspecticide is referred to as the incapacity to know the things you already know, as a result of abuse. It occurs when you lose your grasp on the truth and your sense of self. The narcissist slowly chips away at your perspective until it gets to a point when you get confused and have no thoughts of your own. Prisoners of war have had this psychological manipulation tactic used on them. The goal of this is to make the intended target have a total loss of identity because it is not that difficult to control someone who has no thoughts, feelings, and opinions of their own.

Remember how far you have come on this journey of healing whenever you find yourself going back into the shadows of your loss of self. You are now done tolerating your narcissistic partner's verbal holocaust or snide opinions. You have taken over yourself and won't allow yourself to be their emotional punching bag or receptacle for hatred anymore, because it is over.

Your life is now free of emotional baggage because you have taken the necessary steps to set yourself free from their grasp, and you can now paint a beautiful dream for your future.

Acceptance and Reintegration Phase

You begin to see things clearly and the way they are, and you are now aware of your abilities and your limitations. You have your own thoughts, not the thoughts your ex forced into your mind. At this point, you have the courage to take action when anyone belittles you and treats you badly. You also understand how to develop great and healthy relationships.

Know that narcissists are everywhere, so don't ever lose your sense of wisdom and let your guard down. Ensure that you go all out to stand up to their abuse before the situation gets worse.

From Victim to Survivor

During your recovery, you will pass from being a victim to a survivor.

It is not just enough to learn about narcissists and narcissistic abuse; recovery is much more than that. There are things that you must learn to protect you and help you avoid falling into an abusive relationship with another narcissist.

You must heal the Post Traumatic Stress Disorder (PTSD) you have, and this you can do by learning about yourself, the trauma you experienced right from your childhood, and also learning how to set boundaries. You must do all these if you are ready to heal.

You also have your own issues as to why you remained in the relationship and allowed yourself to be abused. The narcissist treating you bad is only half the story, so the other half of the story is about your own issues.

As a survivor, you need to understand that narcissists never take accountability for anything that is their fault and accept the truth. Their behavior has hurt you, so now you must go all out to protect yourself so that you don't suffer narcissistic abuse again.

Some victims of narcissistic abuse may have had a narcissist family member in the past that basically trained them into accepting this kind of treatment. Keep an open mind to hearing this news if you are just getting to learn more about your past.

Victim Stage

At the victim stage, you might have the following feelings:

Hurt, rejection, confusion, shame, denial, facing betrayal, fear, loneliness, angry at yourself, your narcissist partner or someone else, and victimized by family and friends that think you have lost your mind.

Survivor Stage

When you get to the survivor stage, you will be:

Uncovering childhood trauma that made you a narcissist's victim, Struggling to rebuild your life, getting counseling, rebuilding your financial strength, reevaluating your friendships, not ready to forgive, still having trust issues, depressed, hyper-aware and seeing narcissists everywhere you go, learning techniques for self-soothing, and hopeful.

If you stay determined and ready to do all it takes to heal from the pain associated with the divorce, you will eventually get better, and the emotional and psychological stress the marriage has put you through will be over.

CHAPTER TWELVE

Mistakes Preventing Healing

What you do after a relationship ends is what matters. Are you going to keep being depressed, or are you going to start a new life? It's never easy to end a relationship with someone you have spent part of your life with. After you end a toxic relationship, moving forward should be the only option for you because you don't want to stay stuck in the past.

Don't believe that as soon as you divorce your narcissist spouse, you will heal automatically. Leaving the relationship is not all that is needed. You may even go through some of the most traumatic experiences of your life after the divorce, especially if there are kids involved.

There are mistakes many people make after a divorce that halt recovery, so ensure that you avoid the following recovery mistakes while trying to move forward with your life after the divorce so that you don't get stuck in a vortex of never truly moving on with your life.

Let us take a look at these mistakes.

Reading Endlessly About Narcissistic Traits

If you keep reading endless amounts of information about narcissistic behaviors, and you stay in that negative mindset, your whole mindset will be consumed with narcissism, and your stress levels will increase. To help with your healing, you should stop reading endlessly about narcissistic traits.

Staying Friends

Why would you want to stay friends with someone who hurt you so badly and made your life miserable? Would you be okay with your son or daughter dating someone who makes their life miserable? I guess not. So, it is better not to stay friends with your narcissist ex.

You can't keep them in your life and find a way to manage the abuse; there is no way that can work. The harder you try to manage things so that it can work between you two, the more it fuels them to display more of their narcissistic traits towards you.

Not Accepting the Glaring Fact That Your Ex Is Dangerous To Your Physical and Emotional Health

We hate what we are going through in the marriage to our narcissistic spouse, but we give up and accept that this is how life is; that this is just one of the uncertainties of life. Even though we hate the uncertainties of life, we just give up and say this is how things will remain, and they will never change for the better. It's like we become addicted to the relationship, and our minds make up all kinds of stories about why we can't end the relationship. It's important that we stick to the fact and react based on reality and not based on what our mind just perceives to be the reality.

Your reaction to a situation depends on how you see the situation. If you choose to see it as a tragedy, you will respond accordingly. If you see yourself as someone who is a victim of circumstance, you will remain right there.

Realize that life is a teacher, and we are students of life. Everything happening to us adds to our experience, and our choices and reactions to situations are impacted by our experiences.

If you feel like you always have to prove your worth to your partner, then this should send warning signals to you, so that you can do the right thing for your physical and emotional health.

Having Unrealistic Expectations about How Long the Healing Process Takes

Ending a relationship with a narcissist is different from ending a relationship with anyone else. Most times, we have unrealistic expectations and set unrealistic goals about the speed of our recovery. We are looking for the magic pill that will make us alright again the next morning, and this makes us put ourselves under pressure.

Getting over a relationship that has ended, especially an emotionally abusive one, is a process. You don't just heal magically overnight and get instant restoration. Healing is a journey. The speed of healing varies from individual to individual.

It is possible to have an instant recovery, but it is rare. When we end an abusive relationship, we are left with the damage done to us during the time of the relationship, and this also opens up other issues that have been accumulated over time.

Our healing comes from a combination of small and actionable steps that we take each day, so it takes time. Your relationship with your ex has left you traumatized, so remember to be easy on yourself and show yourself kindness.

Avoiding the Hard Work of Moving On With Your Life Because It Would Bring About a Loss of Identity

Moving on would cause a terrible loss of identity for most people because they are already used to the lifestyle they have now. If you don't want to move on, then you can't; you must want to move on with your life. Many people remain where they are because they are receiving lots of sympathy and attention from family and friends. Since they are down and getting all the sympathy and attention, they get comfortable with remaining where they are. They start feeling like they matter, and this can hinder recovery as they tend to remain in that position to keep receiving attention and sympathy.

Ask yourself if you are ready to heal from the pain of the breakup, and if you are ready to take the needed steps to move forward with your life. You may have really suffered abuse, anxiety, and depression in the relationship. Still, you need to make up your mind and be determined never to sink any lower than that before your transformation and recovery can begin.

Start digging until you hit your rock bottom so that you can make a turn and start recovering from the breakup. You might be saying that you are ready to start the process of recovery, but you are still holding on to the habit of living life with a narcissist and afraid of letting go. It is only when you decide to let go that you will start seeing a change.

Make up your mind and get ready to start living again. You deserve to be loved and respected. You deserve to live a life that is full of happiness and a life that is free from abuse. Ending a toxic relationship can be an opportunity for you to make changes in your life. You can move from your breakup to breakthrough after the marriage ends.

You can have financial freedom and start living a more flourishing life. You can also help others in similar situations. After you have gone through the divorce and healing process, you can help others find their light because you came from a place of darkness, but you found the light within you. Your divorce is actually an opportunity for you to fix the things in your life that weren't working. You get to fix the things that you've been dragging along with you your entire life. It is time to pick up the courage to reinvent yourself.

After the divorce and you have now taken back control, you can do what you didn't have the courage to do while you were in the relationship; you can brush your ex's dirt off your shoulder just as it is landing.

CHAPTER THIRTEEN

Co-Parenting with a Narcissist

Know that you are the adult, and the onus is on you, so see your breakup as your superpower.

You may have gotten pretty good at letting your narcissist ex's attempts fire you up because they keep trying to get under your skin and won't stop. They belittle you for not doing something and then turn around to ridicule you for doing it. They can even withhold child support just so that they can get the opportunity to control you.

You may have taken the bait and allowed yourself to be involved in power struggles, blame games, and unnecessary arguments about who was better at parenting.

You may have found yourself protesting and lecturing your ex about their parental deficiencies when they ruin your plans and break their commitments to the children. You personally respond to their abuse and every ridiculous accusation, wasting your time and energy in the process. However, after doing all these, you will still be where you are, and you would have only succeeded in wasting your valuable time and energy.

What you should know is that the cost of your reactions is too high. The reality is that your ex isn't going to change their behavior anytime soon, and that simply means that you are the sane one who should change yours.

Now, this may be a liberating thing to decide to do, but the change is not going to happen overnight. You need to get to work. You have to work at overriding your thoughts and your behaviors. Once you do this, you will notice that your ex will drop out of your list of most important things. You will handle communications with them maturely, and regulating your own emotions will be easy for you. Your energy will be reserved for your kids and your work, and you will do the things that will make you into the person you have always wanted to be.

Narcissistic abuse is insidious and pervasive, and there will be a point when you don't believe that anything can get better.

There are steps you can take to knock your narcissist's behavior to the bottom of your priority list, and make them undeserving of your energy and attention.

Let us talk about the steps:

Lower Your Expectations

The most important strategy you have at your disposal is lowering your expectations and dealing with what is.

The disappointment you experience when you have unmet expectations is capable of making you miserable. It could be painful to watch your kids not have the kind of co-parent you want them to have.

When you leave, and there is no one to prop them up, everything comes more clearly into focus. It can be shocking to see how deficient they really are.

You find yourself lamenting all the things a good parent would do and wish that you had a similar co-parent who is capable and mature, but the wishes don't get you anywhere.

You will feel disappointed when your partner doesn't show up to co-parent as the child-focused parenting partner you wish you had. However, you will also learn to let go of the disappointment once you are able to realize their capabilities and limitations.

Learning to let go will save you from emotional stress. Your energy will be used for other things because less disappointment will make more energy available that you can use for positive things in your life.

You will end up wasting your energy trying to school them about what a good co-parent should be like, while they keep repeating the same behavior. Once you realize that that is just who they are and they simply can't do those things, you will stop stressing yourself over it. You will stop lamenting all the things they should be capable of and which they aren't.

Remember that your ex is a narcissist, and they are not interested in anything that doesn't align with their self-promotion agenda. The sooner you understand that and come to terms with it, the less energy you will waste on them.

Realize That Their Number One Goal Is To Get Your Attention

Since you were married to your ex, you were their primary source of narcissistic supply, making them addicted to your attention. Be sure that they will say anything or act in any way just to get a reaction from you, but you can break their addiction by withholding your attention from them.

Set Communication Boundaries

Make a decision that you will communicate with your ex only on the following terms:

The topic they are bringing up for communication must be about the children, the request they are making must be a reasonable one, and it must be communicated to you in a polite and reasonable tone. You can also add that all the three requirements must be respected if they truly want a response from you, and if any of the requirements are violated, their email or text message will not be replied. If they violate any of the requirements, then stay true to your word and ignore them. It may be a difficult thing to pull off at first, especially if they have already figured out what to do to trigger a response from you.

Commit To a 24-Hour Turnaround Time on Communications

Take some time before responding to their message. You can wait for 24 hours. Even if you think 24 hours is too long, do it just to let them know that you are not going to be at their beck and call. You can stay longer before responding if you need to, and if they point accusing fingers at you saying you are ignoring them, then let it be so. When you take enough time before responding, it will help you modulate the reactionary content of your replies and keep your emotions in check.

Your ex may have realized that baiting you with false statements may be particularly effective at getting a reaction from you. They will say a few incorrect things to you in a message, and your fingers would literally itch to give them a befitting response. You want to respond because you believe that your non-response was the same as approving of their actions and opinions. Hence, you want to respond and counter their accusations and assignments of blame with the truth and correct information. Your ex already knows how you will react when they do this, so they send you that kind of email to get a reaction from you. When you realize that, you will learn to prioritize depriving them of the attention they are seeking over correcting the record they have sent you via message.

Even if they want to assert that you were late five times in a row when you weren't even late once, just leave it that way. Your silence is not complacency; remember that they aren't even interested in the truth, so whatever they say shouldn't even get your attention.

Realize That Their Statements Have Zero Information Value

Your narcissist isn't trying to co-parent effectively. They may act like they are doing their best while others are watching, but they are only faking it. Nothing they say can be believed and counted on because they are only trying to feed their narcissistic supply. Their communication holds zero information, and they will tell you lies just to manipulate you.

If they promise that they will be somewhere at 11 am, and they find a way to get the attention that precludes them from being at that place by 11 am, they won't show up at 11 am because it won't serve their purpose anymore, so their promises actually mean nothing.

Don't make the mistake of thinking that their email saying they will pick the children up at 4 pm actually means that they will do just that because if they can find a way to get into an argument with you and get the attention they crave for, the statement they made in writing will be neglected in favor of an attempt to control you. Their commitments mean nothing, and their statements have zero information value, so don't believe them.

Reverse Pronouns

This method is effective when you are trying to regulate your emotions in response to your ex's abuse and accusations. Narcissists are emotional children, and they are also masters of projection.

For example, when they write, "you are the worst mom", realize that they are really saying, "I am the worst dad". They can say, "your children will grow up hating you", but what they are really saying is, "my children will grow up hating me".

When you understand this, you will be able to resist the urge to reply to their baiting abuse and accusations.

Narcissists are emotional children, and most of them developed these habits when they were children, making it a part of them; this is what makes it so difficult for them to be aware of their behavior so that they can develop the capacity to change it.

They have huge egos that seem to be constructed to keep them alive, so they will always be children in grown-up bodies.

You may not see your ex as a child, but the truth is that they have similar behavior with children; pay attention, and you will see the similarities. They crave constant attention and like to be praised, they throw tantrums when they don't have their way, they test boundaries, and they are also self-centered.

The only way you can handle their behavior is to set boundaries like you would when dealing with a child. You have to be persistent with boundaries and consequences and make them experience the consequences of violating your rules.

Remember, their content has zero information, so do your best to ignore their protest tantrums and engaging in a power struggle with them.

Do What Works For You

Notify your ex that communication with them will be only through email if you discover that answering their phone calls always ends up in a fight.

If they also demand to change the pickup time for the kids or visitation schedule without giving you a reasonable explanation, only accept the new arrangement if it works for you. It is crucial that you remember this because if you give in to their demands, they will keep bombarding you with demands, and they will never stop.

You can only accept their demands if it works for you, and it is on your terms. Ensure that you make the decisions because you are the parent here.

Accept That You Can Depend On Them for Nothing

Get used to the fact that your ex can miss pickups and payments. They may owe you child support, medical expenses, or even visitation, but don't count on them for any of that. Just assume they won't do any of that so that you don't keep expecting something that they are not thinking of doing. If they do it, it's fine, but if they don't, it's also fine.

Don't panic and get upset; just learn to make other arrangements beforehand to make up for the times they don't keep to their promises. Ensure that you depend on them for nothing.

You Are the Grown-up

Make the decision about what works and what doesn't. Don't ask for their opinion on anything. You are the only grown up in the equation who needs to oversee things, so true co-parenting is impossible with a narcissist. Your ex is all tied up in his own needs and isn't capable of putting the needs of the children first.

Pay Attention to Your Children's Feelings

Having a narcissistic parent can be traumatic for a child, especially if child custody is being shared 50/50. When you are not present, be sure that your ex can even selfishly use the child to meet their own needs. This is the heart-breaking truth, so while you may be fighting for the court to grant you full custody, you only have the power to control whatever happens in your house. This is why it is crucial for you to make your home emotionally safe for your children.

When you pick your kids up from your ex's house, you can ask them how they spent their time and listen to them. Ensure that you give them emotional support and not judging them, or they will stop talking to you about things. Give them time to express their feelings and let them know that they are safe with you. Make yourself a safe place for your kids.

Don't badmouth your ex in front of the kids. Resist the urge to do it as it will only leave them confused.

It is also good for you to be familiar with the laws regarding when the children can make decisions for themselves whether they want to exercise visitation. The oldest child may decide they don't want to see your ex if they perceive their self-centeredness and manipulation attempts. The other children may also decide to follow in the steps of the oldest child and also decide not to see your ex if their behavior doesn't change for the better.

When the kids start telling your ex what part of their behavior they must change to reestablish a relationship with them, your ex will make up a story blaming you instead of taking responsibility and making the requested changes in their behavior.

Both parents indeed play an important role in the lives of the children. Still, when kids get to a certain stage in their lives, they have the right to decide whether the relationship with a narcissistic parent works for them or not because the abusive behavior of a narcissistic parent can cause great damage to a child's emotional well-being. When kids become old enough to make a decision, they sometimes choose "no contact" after going through counseling sessions to help them decide what they truly want. It is vital that they make the best decision for their emotional well-being so that they can be happy.

Stop Worrying About What Other People Think

Most mental health professionals have to speak with family members before they can identify a narcissist. Don't go expecting your ex's family who are the ones that created the pathology, and their friends, who are the ones actively enabling it to suddenly see that the truth is a fantasy. Realize that your ex will paint you as the devil to anyone who cares to listen to them.

Narcissists fabricate stories about how poorly you treat them to feed their ego. They can't dare to lose their pity and victim status. Their positive feelings come from what other people think and say about them. Ensure that you stay away from people that are vulnerable to your ex's influence and buy into their lies unquestioned because you don't need such people in your life.

Report Abuse

There is a line, and it is crucial that you know when it has been crossed. Ensure that you don't ignore threats; take them seriously, document them, and report abuse. For your safety, it is best for you to report anything at all that is reportable. Don't ever tolerate any kind of threat.

Ensure that you defend and protect the kids at all costs. Narcissists can get you baited into arguments if they succeed at pressing the right button. They will try until they find a weakness to hold on to. They are naturally good at this, so don't put yourself under any pressure and beat yourself up when you make any mistakes.

You may be far more intelligent than your ex, but their pathology may be smarter than you. You might have left the relationship a long time ago if you didn't have children with them, but now that you have children with them, you have to face the reality of sharing custody with the absence of the "No Contact" option.

You keep wishing that you had a grown-up co-parent that will support you and the children, but that is the price you have to pay for choosing to marry a narcissist. The only thing left for you to do is to take responsibility and put in the needed work to save you and your children from future setbacks and pain. Taking responsibility will benefit your children and also empower you.

It is never easy co-parenting with a narcissist, but by divorcing them, you have taken a giant step towards taking control of your life and having a better future. Your children deserve the very best of you, so reserve your energy for them. You cannot be wasting your energy on your narcissistic ex and trying to cope with the emotional stress they are trying to put you through just to serve their own needs when you should be putting your energy into caring for you and the kids. Ensure that you protect yourself and keep your resources safe. Change your negative thoughts and stay focused on positivity.

You will find it difficult at first, but if you commit to the process, dealing with your ex will get easier, and you will eventually heal from the pain.

CHAPTER FOURTEEN

Finding Yourself

After breaking free from a narcissistic relationship, years later you may still feel like you have lost yourself as a result. The process of self-recovery and discovery can be long and grueling.

There may be no time stamp on the amount of time it takes to re-discover the self that you have lost, but it is still possible for you to find yourself. There is still life ahead of you and it is an opportunity for you to become the person you have always wanted to be. Even though you now feel like you are broken and left alone without any sense of purpose, you can still become the person you have always dreamed of becoming.

Here is what you should do:

Acknowledge the Role You Played In the Relationship

You have been mistreated and abused in the relationship, but it is because you allowed the abuse to happen. You were too weak and afraid to leave the relationship so you had to put up with your narcissistic partner's damaging behavior for years. You played a role in this relationship and you may have done it out of the love you have for your spouse, but you must first acknowledge the part you played in the relationship so that you can move on in life and into your next step of healing, which is forgiveness.

Forgive Yourself and Forgive Your Ex

First of all, you must forgive yourself. After acknowledging the role you played in the relationship, it is time to stop judging yourself over everything that happened. Stop punishing your emotions more. People make mistakes in life every day and it isn't something new. Whatever you are going through today, someone must have passed through a similar situation. Accept the fact that we all make mistakes, but it is what we do after the mistakes we have made that defines who we are.

Secondly, you need to forgive your ex. You can still remember what they did to you to make you careful about your next relationship. Realize that they are just the way they are. A cat will always be a cat. You mustn't associate yourself with them, but you need to let go so that you can move on with your life. Forgive them for the way they have behaved towards you because it is just who they are. You both made a bad combination so use what you have learnt from the relationship to improve your life and never let yourself fall for your ex or any person with similar behavior ever again.

Avoid Taking Over the Voice of the Narcissist

After you have ended the relationship, refuse to take over the voice of the narcissist in your head. The voice will prevent you from moving on with your life. When you spend years living with a narcissist, you become conditioned to a specific way of reasoning. This is why it is crucial that you change your inner voice. Guard your thoughts so that whenever they take you to the hurtful and self-destructive place, work on taking your thoughts to a happy place by focusing on the moment and practicing gratitude instead.

Don't Pressure Yourself to Reach a Goal of Self-Discovery

Stop focusing too much on self-discovery. When you do this, you take the narcissist's place in your life by telling yourself that you are not doing well and you are failing at self-discovery. You are already who you are, and whether you know who that is or not, it doesn't change who you are. That doesn't matter. What matters is your ability to focus on what's good in your life and not magnify the problem areas. You will add more to your sorrow if you maintain self-pity and prolonged grief over a self you think you have lost. You will end up ruining your present.

The road to recovery after a divorce is a long one. Life is not a race involving who gets to the finish line first, so there is no need to be in a hurry; just take your time.

It is best that you loosen your grip on yourself, practice self-care, and allow yourself to heal gradually.

CHAPTER FIFTEEN

The Mirror Theory

When someone comes into our lives, they often come to show us something about ourselves.

How did you act toward yourself before attracting a narcissist into your life? Are you neglecting yourself or having no regard for yourself? Do you feel that you are far better than everyone else? Do you say things about others and put them down when you feel insecure so that you can feel better about yourself?

You may not have all the narcissistic traits, but you may have attracted a narcissist into your life because some of those traits are in you. Ask yourself a question about what traits cause you the most problems even though all the narcissistic traits are not mirrored in you. Then you can ask yourself how you subconsciously attracted a narcissist into your life.

You need to change your mindset from that of a victim to owning your own life. It may be difficult for you to understand this idea. Because you have been hurt by a narcissist and you feel less confident about yourself, you may keep blaming yourself for remaining in the relationship for too long before putting an end to it.

People who got divorced from narcissists often find themselves bruised emotionally and carrying along their victim mentality. They were courageous enough to leave their narcissistic spouse, but may still become abusive towards themselves and display the narcissistic tendencies they walked away from.

Focus on You

You may be focusing on your narcissistic ex and the experiences you had with them, but it is also necessary that you focus on yourself and learn the needed lessons from the experience. It will help you move on and never repeat the experience again.

Since narcissists have a constant need to make themselves look better than others. They have a profound lack of self-esteem hiding underneath their apparent self-confidence. They are more inclined to choose a partner who doubts themselves and their capabilities because they want to make themselves feel better.

A narcissist wouldn't choose a partner that has strong self-esteem and confidence in themselves because they enjoy power and like to be the ones in control. A person with a healthy self-confidence who enters into a relationship with a narcissist, quickly recognizes the emotional abuse and puts an end to the relationship. They recognize that all is not well and they can't be in such a relationship. Once they realize this, they focus on themselves and quickly leave an unhappy relationship that is of no value to them.

Stop Judging Yourself

You make yourself the perfect target for a narcissist as soon as you start doubting yourself and displaying a lack of confidence.

Narcissists display confidence, strength, and they appear appealing when you first get to know them because they aim to reel you in with their charms and make you think it is all about you.

If all the attention they were giving to you didn't confuse you and you didn't doubt yourself, you would have discovered in time that they were only coming close to you because you appeared weak and could be their victim. I'm sure you wouldn't have even started a relationship with them if you had known this right from the beginning.

Before you start a new relationship, you should ask yourself these questions: how can i stop myself from sending signals of neediness and that I need a savior who will give me lots of attention? How can I look after myself better?

Stop any relationship with a narcissist just as it is beginning. By believing in yourself, you will nip it in the bud. When you pay proper attention to yourself and have a healthy self-esteem, you won't attract anyone who has the ability to spot a potential partner with low self-esteem for their own personal gain.

Narcissistic traits can be exceptional if used appropriately and personal boundaries are respected. Narcissistic traits could make people exceptional. Narcissistic traits like ambition or even desire for power could be good attributes when balanced with humility and used for the good of others. It is not a bad thing to be powerful, but when you start putting others down because of your need to feel powerful, then it becomes an issue.

The First Clue

The reason you attracted a narcissist may be because you lack confidence. In the beginning of the relationship did you ever wonder why such a great person was choosing to date you? That was the first clue you had.

Something peculiar to relationships with narcissists is that there is often an imbalance between them and the people they are in a relationship with. They date people who appear much more ordinary as they are superficially exceptional people.

An obvious imbalance in attributes or personality where one partner is highly extroverted and the other partner is highly introverted sets alarm bells ringing. Narcissists are highly exceptional in their own minds. Their victims are often the successful ones, but they tend to disappear in the shadow of the pretender.

Remember that you are a special person and probably more successful than you believe. Since narcissists are quite picky, they don't go into a relationship with just anybody, they take their time to search for people who are successful and accomplished and who are also kind enough to let them reign supreme and over shadow them.

It's time to stop allowing the narcissist to turn your lack of self-confidence into an opportunity to treat you badly; stop downplaying and underrating yourself. Embrace your new life and the truth about yourself, so you can rise again.

Now that you have left the abusive relationship behind by replacing the negative thoughts that held you down with more positive thoughts, you can gradually rebuild your self-confidence by allowing yourself to heal and grow into the positive person you want to be. Learn to believe in yourself and be your own leader.

CHAPTER SIXTEEN

When It Is Over

The road to healing after divorcing a narcissist can be likened to a rollercoaster in a washing machine set on spin; it isn't a straight and easy one. This is because narcissistic abuse is like psychological warfare that messes your entire mind, heart, and soul. You will travel the long and difficult road of healing after divorcing the narcissist that turned your life upside down. It takes courage and determination for you to make it to the other side.

However, you can make your journey to healing faster and achieve the emotional freedom you need. There is a map to guide you on this journey to claim your space in the light and leave the darkness behind for good.

Let us discuss the things you must do while healing from narcissistic abuse.

Stop Checking On Social Media

Social media will slow down your healing process if you keep checking on your ex. Social media could be an enemy to your healing process if you let it. There are people who could ruin your day by simply reminding you of the pain you are going through. You may find it tempting to check on your ex and see what they are up to, but it will only leave you worse off and not better off, so don't do it.

It is better to stay off their social media page because narcissists will post events showing their great new life without you and act like they are so happy without you in their life, but in reality, they are really not happy without you. They just want to do something that will take away the shame of the divorce and maintain their self-image.

They can also bombard you with messages about pleas of getting back together that they are now changed, but be wise and realize that narcissists never change.

The best way to avoid this nightmare is to unfollow, unfriend, block, and delete them on social media so that you don't get tempted into stalking them.

Empower Yourself

Empowering yourself through your own education about what exactly a narcissist is and what constitutes abuse is important. Many victims have never heard about narcissistic personality disorder and do not realize they are victims of narcissistic abuse until much later in the relationship when they have already suffered so much. Because they have no broken bones or bruises, they remain feeling isolated and alone without realizing they are married to a narcissist.

Once you educate yourself about narcissists and narcissistic abuse, you will be able to put a name to your pain and realize that you were normal all along and wasn't the crazy one after all. Being able to name the problem is the first step towards fixing it, and putting yourself on the road to taking power back from your abuser.

Stay Away From People Who Are Not 100% On Your Side

You are sensitive and emotional when you are healing, and people who do not have your best interests at heart can easily prey on your vulnerability.

Sometimes, the people we least expect end up deserting us in our time of need. It is necessary that you keep away people who are not 100% on your side; people who are holding you back from moving forward with your life. It is time to stay away from anyone who sits on the fence about your situation with your partner with the "I don't want to get involved with this" attitude.

Their intentions are wholly self-serving, so keep such people away from your life. They are not worth taking on this journey with you.

You can start by finding out the people you should keep out of your life. Watch them closely and study how you feel when you are with them. Do you feel like you have to defend yourself or do you feel safe and comfortable with them? Do you feel better or worse off whenever you meet them? Your instincts will tell you when someone is completely on your side and when they aren't. Keep those you feel good around and do away with the ones you don't feel good around.

Don't Block Out The Past

It is a good thing for you to spend time reflecting on your past and see the steps you took that led you to where you are now. Reflecting on your past doesn't mean that you have to look back and blame yourself for everything that you suffered from your narcissistic abuser; it only helps you figure out how you ended up marrying them so that you don't ignore signs of such behavior in future relationships and repeat the same mistakes you made.

This is a tough part of healing because you will have to look back on your past. You will discover why you had some issues and why you had to put up with your narcissistic ex for so long and allowed yourself to be an object of their control.

If you ignore your past, you do so at your own peril. When you travel back into your future to figure things out, you will understand what happened every step of the way and then make peace with yourself. This way, you will strip your past of the power to destroy your future.

Do Not Jump Into a New Relationship

Starting a new relationship right after a divorce is a mistake. You will still be in a vulnerable state and can be easily preyed on by a new person coming into your life. The worst mistake you can make after divorcing a narcissist is to jump right into another relationship because you want someone to be a shoulder for you to cry on. You may still have a twisted view of things because of what you went through in the hands of your ex, so you can't see clearly to select a good mate. It is common for victims who have just escaped narcissistic abuse to have low self-worth. Starting a new relationship at this time will just be like someone driving with their eyes closed.

You need some time to yourself; time to reflect, grieve, cry or do anything to help you calm your nerves. Happiness lies within you. If you look within yourself, you will avoid the risk of falling for someone else who may turn out to be another bad news like your ex.

Ignore Your Ex

We know that narcissists thrive on drama, and it seems like their only objective is to suck the life out of anyone with a beating heart. They will portray this in your communications with them if you still have any with them after divorce.

If you still go on responding to their allegations and defending yourself against something they've accused you of, you are opening up the door slightly for them to push it open and come right back into your life. Every time your vampire ex is thirsty for blood, you must ignore them and keep your eyes on the road forward instead of applying the brakes to attend to them.

Don't give a narcissist what they are looking for. Don't give them the reaction they are after. They don't care about the kind of reaction; all they care about is getting a reaction that they can use in mocking you so that they can win.

Let It Go

The first thing to do is to figure out the exact thing you are not forgiving yourself for and write it down. If you have been keeping a lot of things in your mind and don't really like the person you have become, this is the right time to forgive yourself and let it go.

This part of the journey will be hard for you because you must have already gotten used to the person you have become and have been blaming yourself for things you have done as a result of your ex's behavior.

Pretend that it's someone you love who is saying this to you. If they came and said "I am so mad at myself for not standing up for myself and for allowing myself to be abused!" What would you tell the person? What words of consolation would you say to them? I'm sure you would say something like, "don't worry honey, the abuse wasn't your fault at all; everything will be alright". You would then give them a hug and add that they should consider those years spent with their narcissistic ex a period of learning and growing that they should look ahead to the bright future and then live their life with happiness.

The thing is that you would show them love and advise them to forgive themselves. So, go ahead and figure out why it's difficult for you to forgive yourself then take your own advice and move on with your life. Set yourself free from the feelings of guilt and shame that is holding you back from stepping into the future you want for yourself; doing this will give you emotional freedom and healing from the narcissistic abuse.

Take the driver's seat and be in control of your life. Forgive yourself for your past mistakes and give your self-worth a chance.

Conclusion

The narcissist can easily put their crimes and sin into a box inside their brain and then go ahead to label the box "not my fault" or "someone else's fault". Normal people are unable to do this because they have a conscience that convicts them of their crimes and sinful behavior. Most narcissists do not have an active conscience; their conscience may have been hardened from many years of denying it, or they didn't even have it in the first place.

Narcissists compartmentalize and rationalize their sin, and they are able to continue with what they were doing without feeling remorseful when compartmentalizing the sin.

Lying is easy for them as they believe that they weren't to blame. Narcissists put everything they have done and all their lies into the same box consisting of their excuses.

They can create a storyline and repeat it over and over again; they will also deviate from it as needed when narrating it to different parties. The narcissist believes in their mind that the story they have created is actually the truth. It wasn't their fault that something happened; it was their victim that did that to themselves.

A narcissist may try coming back to their ex in the future, but once their ex has gone through the long hard road to recovery and moved on with their life, they are no more the narcissist's victim. Once "No Contact" has been established and stronger boundaries put in place, the right of being the narcissist's victim that they assigned to themselves is revoked, and this prevents the narcissist from ever coming back into their life to control them.

When they come back in the future because they can't let you go, they will find out that you have become a completely different person that cannot be manipulated and used.

It is advisable that you don't allow the narcissist to know your intentions ahead of time. They will probably get outraged, and may even become violent, and you need to get prepared for that. They feel you are not allowed to leave them without their permission because they own you, so carefully take out time to plan how you will go about the divorce. Ensure that you save all the money you can in a personal account that they have no idea exists because you are going to need the money.

You can go to a domestic violence/abuse center and get all the information you can from them. When you finally get divorced, they know how to help you stay safe and away from your ex.

Remember to do this before you serve them the divorce because as soon as you file and they get served, the fun starts. Don't expect your partner to be fair or believe them when they say you two can work things out. They will definitely make promises, but it is all talk that they will never act on.

Protect yourself. You can also request police protection if you are going to leave the house and need to go back to get your possessions.

Remember that narcissists are capable of hiding all the important documents, including your own birth certificate. They can even take out loans in your name and should not be trusted at all.

What you need is the courage to go through the divorce. With proper planning and a support system in place, you will go through it and move on with your life.